A BERLIN REPUBLIC

A Berlin Republic: Writings on Germany

Die Normalität einer Berliner Republik

JÜRGEN HABERMAS

Translated by Steven Rendall

Introduction by Peter Uwe Hohendahl

University of Nebraska Press

Lincoln

Publication of this book was assisted by a grant from Inter Nationes, Bonn.
The publisher thanks Michael Roloff for his efforts on behalf of this project.
Originally published as *Die Normalität einer Berliner Republik,* © Suhrkamp Verlag, Frankfurt am Main, 1995. Translation and introduction © 1997 by the University of Nebraska Press. All rights reserved. Manufactured in the United States of America. ⊗ The paper in this book meets the minimum requirements of American National Standard for Information Sciences – Permanence of Paper for Printed Library Materials, ANSI Z39.48-1984
Typeset in Berkeley. Book design by RE.

Library of Congress Cataloging in Publication Data
Habermas, Jürgen. [Normalität einer Berliner Republik. English] A Berlin Republic: writings on Germany / Jürgen Habermas; translated by Steven Rendall; introduction by Peter Uwe Hohendahl. p. cm. – (Modern German culture and literature)
Includes bibliographical references and index.
ISBN 0-8032-2381-1 (cloth: alk. paper) – ISBN 0-8032-7306-1 (paper: alk. paper) 1. Germany – Historiography 2. Germany – History – Philosophy. 3. Germany – History – Unification, 1990. 4. Germany – Intellectual life 5. Political culture – Germany. 6. Germany – Foreign relations – 1945- I. Title II. Series
DD290.24.H313 1997 943.087'9–dc21 97-9486 CIP

Contents

Introduction by Peter Uwe Hohendahl vii

Preface 1

1 CAN WE LEARN FROM HISTORY? 3

2 A DOUBLE PAST

What Does 'Working Off the Past' Mean
Today? 17

Replies to Questions from a Bundestag
Investigative Commission 41

3 GERMAN UNCERTAINTIES

French Views, French Anxieties:
An Interview with *Le Monde* 59

The Germans' 'Sense of Being Special'
Is Regenerating Hour by Hour: An
Interview with the *Frankfurter Rundschau* 69

The Adenauer Restoration's Debts:
An Interview with the *Kölner Stadtanzeiger* 83

4 THE NEED FOR GERMAN CONTINUITIES

A Letter to Christa Wolf 95

Carl Schmitt in the Political Intellectual
History of the Federal Republic 107

Das Falsche im Eigenen: On Benjamin
and Adorno 119

5 BETWEEN FACTS AND NORMS

A Conversation about Questions of
Political Theory 131

6 WHICH HISTORY CAN WE LEARN FROM?

1989 in the Shadow of 1945: On the
Normality of a Future Berlin Republic 161

Index 183

Introduction by Peter Uwe Hohendahl

THE SERIES OF ESSAYS, articles, and interviews collected in this volume reflects a side of Jürgen Habermas's work that is less known in the United States than his major theoretical texts, beginning with *Knowledge and Human Interest* (1971) and leading up to *The Theory of Communicative Action* (1984). They demonstrate the author's ongoing involvement in the German and European public sphere. More specifically, they are the interventions of a passionate public intellectual, who has always felt that his academic appointment at the University of Frankfurt could not be the only platform from which to respond to the questions of the day. The recent discovery of Habermas's early work in the English-speaking world, in particular the publication of *The Structural Transformation of the Public Sphere* in 1989 (the first German edition appeared in 1962), provides perhaps a more suitable frame for an appreciation of the rhetoric of these essays than his theoretically more abstract later writings, as much as they exhibit, although in different forms, their author's strong commitment to the idea of political praxis.[1] Habermas's concept of the public sphere, a space where private persons come together to develop a critical discourse that aims at a rational consensus in matters of culture and politics, still guides the thrust of Habermas's essays from the early 1990s. Al-

1. For a general introduction see Thomas McCarthy, *The Critical Theory of Jürgen Habermas* (Cambridge: MIT Press, 1978); see also *Habermas and Modernity*, ed. Richard J. Bernstein (Cambridge: MIT Press, 1985).

though he moved away from the specific historical arguments of *Structural Transformation* during the 1970s and later completely abandoned the theoretical framework of his first major book, Habermas holds on to the conception of the public sphere as a realm that is not occupied by symbolic media; a realm, in other words, where citizens through the form of rational discussion find the resources to resist the pressure and the intrusion of the state and the economy. In the terminology of Habermas's later work, the public sphere is an essential part of the lifeworld in which people interact and make sense of their lives.

In the new introduction to the 1990 German edition of *Structural Transformation* (available in English as 'Further Reflections on the Public Sphere') Habermas insists again on the need for a vibrant and open public sphere but also on the need for a new and different theoretical grounding. 'I suggested, therefore, that the normative foundations of the critical theory of society be laid at a deeper level. The theory of communicative action intends to bring into the open the rational potential intrinsic in everyday communicative practices.' The part of his early theory he now rejects is the assumption that modern society can be conceived as a large association 'in which the associated individuals can participate like the members of an encompassing organization.'[2] Such an assumption is no longer plausible in a highly complex, functionally differentiated society. Thus Habermas sees the role of the public sphere and that of the intellectual operating within this space in a more pragmatic light than in the 1960s when the utopian element of his theory was decidedly stronger. Whereas the early Habermas hoped for

2. Jürgen Habermas, 'Further Reflections on the Public Sphere,' in *Habermas and the Public Sphere,* ed. Craig Calhoun (Cambridge: MIT Press), 442, 443.

a radical democracy that would reconstruct both the forms and the means of political communication that had led to the decline of the bourgeois public sphere, the Habermas of the 1990s focuses on the moral and legal issues involved in the making of a democratic society. Hence, in his role as a public intellectual he is particularly concerned with questions of political culture and broader issues of historical traditions that transcend the level of conventional party politics. In the revised definition of his task, he foregrounds a moment that was already part of his early theory – political discourse is understood as a form of communication that is not exclusively defined in terms of interests.

As suggested above, Habermas holds on to the ideas of a radical democracy in which the citizens are encouraged to participate in the policy- and decision-making process. Although the state and its various administrative organizations are acknowledged as necessary media of power, they are also viewed as potential threats to democracy. In this respect Habermas stands in sharp contrast to neoconservative intellectuals in Germany, who were influenced by the teachings of Carl Schmitt after 1945 (although Schmitt was not allowed to return to his university post). Schmitt, who had been a crucial political theorist in favor of the takeover by the National Socialists in 1933, continued to have, as Habermas points out in 'Carl Schmitt in the Political Intellectual History of the Federal Republic,' a significant impact on West Germany's intellectual life through private circles and devoted followers, many of whom later ended up in important public positions. For the position of the neoconservatives, the centrality of the state remains unquestioned.

Against this interpretation of the German tradition Habermas wants to foreground the popular and democratic elements of the German past. Yet Habermas's idea of a radical democracy has to be distinguished from two competing versions of political practice; namely, the tradition of communal democracy (Rousseau) on the one hand and state Socialism on the other. Already, in *Structural Transformation,* Habermas had opted for a Kantian reading of the public sphere rather than a populist definition à la Rousseau in which rational deliberation among the citizens as a mode of reaching consensus is played down. Habermas's emphasis on solidarity does not mean a democracy of the heart. More important in the contemporary debate, however, is his opposition to the model of state Socialism, which Habermas encountered in East Germany. Unlike other members of the Left in West Germany, Habermas never showed any sympathy for the version of democratic centralism practiced in East Berlin. Its method of state and party control clearly clashed with Habermas's notion of a democratic process from below based on the deliberations of the citizens. In 1962, Habermas had criticized the lack of a vital political culture in contemporary Western democracies (using primarily American data). He noted a growing fusion of state and parliament, a process that resulted in political decisions based on compromise rather than rational debate. But although Habermas has continued to be a critical observer of parliamentary democracy, he has never suggested or argued for a fundamental change of the West German (now German) constitution. In other words, his notion of radical democracy has been grounded in the liberal tradition that he found in Western Europe and the United States. In his essays, Habermas again and again highlights the historical moment of 1945 as the crucial turning point in German history, when West Germany's political culture took in the ideas of the European Enlightenment. This is precisely the point where he disagrees with Christa Wolf's reading of 1989 in which she emphasized the need to return to the roots of German culture both in the East and in the West. Habermas clearly does not trust an unqualified use of the concept of the German tradition as it has increasingly resurfaced in Germany after 1989.

Habermas's discomfort with the revival of Carl Schmitt and the growing influence of his work after the German reunification in 1990 is closely related to his concern about the antidemocratic elements within the German political tradition. Schmitt's critique of liberal democracy as an outdated form of decision making and his outspoken contempt for deliberative forms of politics are part of a problematic German legacy that Habermas perceives as a danger for the changing political culture of the new German Republic.[3] For Habermas, Schmitt stands close to Martin Heidegger. What they both have in common is a Catholic background – including its traditional critique of the Enlightenment and modernity in general – leading to their decision in 1933 to welcome Hitler as the leader of a new Germany. Neither Heidegger nor Schmitt ever expressed regrets about their commitment in 1933. This attitude, Habermas argues, has then resulted in a reading of German history that has become particularly relevant after 1989 in the work of historians such as Ernst Nolte.[4] It de-emphasizes the collapse of German fascism in

3. See Carl Schmitt, *The Crisis of Parliamentary Democracy* (Cambridge: MIT Press, 1985), originally published in German in 1923, and Carl Schmitt, *Political Theology: Four Chapters on the Concept of Sovereignty* (Cambridge: MIT Press, 1985), originally published in German in 1922.

4. See Ernst Nolte, *Das Vergehen der Vergangenheit* (Frankfurt am Main: Ullstein, 1987); *Lehrstück oder Tragödie? Beiträge zur Interpretationder Ge-

1945 and stresses the need for a return to older political traditions. In his comparison between Theodor Maunz, the leading jurist of the Federal Republic, and Carl Schmitt, Habermas highlights the power and potential danger of Schmitt's thought in Germany: 'But of these two men only Carl Schmitt, only the one who defied the ruling political culture and dramatized himself as a defamed dissident, can make available the resources from which the re-awakened need for German continuities can be satisfied.'

After receiving his Ph.D. in philosophy Habermas began his academic career as the assistant of Theodor W. Adorno in the new Institute for Social Research in Frankfurt. Adorno's influence on the early work of Habermas is hard to overlook. As much as he later moved away from the theoretical foundations of the first generation of the Frankfurt School and increasingly distanced himself from its critique of Enlightenment rationalism, he always stressed his personal loyalties to Adorno and the latter's importance in postwar Germany. Adorno offered a model of intellectual analysis in the public sphere that undoubtedly shaped Habermas's sense of his own project. Adorno, together with Max Horkheimer, Herbert Marcuse, Walter Benjamin, Leo Löwenthal, and Hannah Arendt, embodied the other side of the German tradition – the side that was forced into exile in 1933 and then only reluctantly readmitted in 1945. What Habermas admires in Adorno's writings is a critical appreciation of the German tradition – a deep sympathy and an unquestionable commitment without the nationalistic overtones that

schichte des 20. Jahrhunderts (Cologne: Bölau, 1991); *Die Deutschen und ihre Vergangenheit: Erinnerung und Vergessen von der Reichsgründung Bismarcks bis heute* (Berlin: Propylaen, 1995).

distorted this tradition already in the late nineteenth century. His essay on the exchange of letters between Adorno and Benjamin demonstrates how close Habermas has remained to the legacy of his mentors. It is Adorno rather than Benjamin who is invoked as the intellectual guide and *Praeceptor Germaniae:* 'Adorno made a generation of assistants, one or two generations of students and an eager-to-learn public that read his essays and listened to his radio talks, aware of the silencings and marginalized potentialities, the alienated and encapsulated elements within *our own* traditions.' Hence the end of the essay returns to Habermas's major concerns: the interpretation of the German cultural tradition, its selection and emphasis, and articulates a growing discomfort with the cultural as well as political climate of the new Germany.

This passionate defense of Adorno and the political culture of the 1960s and 1970s shows Habermas in a 'conservative' position – the last defender of the Adenauer Republic, to quote Ralf Dahrendorf. This quip brings into the foreground Habermas's ambivalent attitude toward the early years of the Federal Republic. On the one hand, Adenauer achieved the integration of West Germany into the Western alliance (for Habermas clearly a moment of substantial historical progress). On the other hand, Adenauer's political system remained repressive and refused to come to terms with the German past. The turn of 1945 therefore remained incomplete. For Habermas, it was Critical Theory and the New Left as it emerged in the 1960s that completed this turn. Hence, in his essay 'What Does "Working Off the Past" Mean Today?' Habermas not only invokes Adorno's legacy but also emphasizes his dialectical method; namely, a form of immanent critique that brings to light the repressed elements of the past and thereby makes possible their critical appropriation. Habermas has consistently intervened where he observes attempts to paste over the Third Reich and restore a sense of normal continuity from Bismarck to Kohl. Because these revisionist voices have become stronger during the last decade and have also found more prominent media (among them the *Frankfurter Allgemeine Zeitung*), the critique of historical revisionism has become a constant theme in Habermas's writings since the Historians' Debate in 1986.[5] Since 1989, however, these issues have penetrated German political culture to a much higher degree. The quest for a common national identity caused by the unexpected and hasty act of unification undermined the Left-liberal consensus of the intellectuals and the political class in West Germany (not to mention the disastrous results for the intelligentsia in East Germany). Now Germany's integration into the West appeared in a different light; namely, as her potential participation in global political power and a possible renewal of hegemony in Europe.[6]

Habermas's response to these tendencies has been decidedly critical. He has rejected both the claim for a new foreign policy exclusively based on principles of national self-interest and military power that would be demonstrated through international actions and economic pressure, and he has sharply criticized the potential erosion of democratic rights in the changing political structure of post-Wall Germany. The increasing violence against foreigners in the early

5. See Charles Maier, *The Unmasterable Past* (Cambridge: Harvard University Press, 1988).

6. On the changes in the public sphere in post-Wall Germany see Peter Uwe Hohendahl, 'Recasting the Public Sphere,' *October* 73 (summer 1995), 27–54.

1990s, the curtailment of the right of asylum guaranteed by the Basic Law of the Federal Republic, as well as the attempts of the Federal government and the states (Länder) to increase the power of the police vis-à-vis the citizens are prominent examples of the new climate that Habermas mentions. In this context he points to the moral ground of the legal system and especially of the constitution, which is supposed to protect the individual citizen. 'The legal order of democratic constitutional states embodies a moral content, and for the realization of that content it is not dependent solely on the goodwill of those whom it addresses.' He continues to argue that the democratic procedures as they are presumed by the German constitution depend on active citizens. To put it differently, they depend on exchange of ideas and debate in a functioning public sphere. Habermas wants to assert (and this may seem radical only against the background of a conservative German tradition) that a legitimate legal system cannot exist without moral foundations and democratic procedures.

For Habermas, radical democracy is a procedural democracy – a definition that differs from a type of representative democracy in which popular participation is limited to a few formal acts such as voting.[7] The Habermasian emphasis on procedures indicates that it is difficult to establish consensus in a modern society where its members no longer automatically share the same worldview (religion). It is apparent that Habermas is not satisfied with the procedures of party democracy (which Germany's constitution favors) and encourages free associations and Bürgerinitiativen as venues

7. See also Seyla Benhabib, 'Models of Public Space: Hannah Arendt, the Liberal Tradition, and Jürgen Habermas,' in Habermas and the Public Sphere, 73–98.

for critical exchange and political deliberation. In the German case, the dilemma seems to be, however, that the public sphere, in which this form of basic democracy has to be rooted, has increasingly been occupied by neoconservative ideas that are hardly compatible with the concept of a radical democracy. For these intellectuals, not 1945 but 1989 is the true turning point of German history; namely, the restoration of Germany's 'normal' position as a major political power in Europe that selects and carries out policies according to its own national interests (which are those of the state rather than those of the citizens).

For his conservative opponents and critics, Habermas's attitude toward the unification of Germany and, more broadly, German nationalism has been particularly frustrating. Not only did he resist the widespread enthusiasm for unification, but he also repeatedly took issue with the new wave of nationalism in East and West.[8] Instead, he stressed the need for a different form of patriotism at the end of the twentieth century. His call for *Verfassungspatriotismus* (constitutional patriotism) focused on the centrality of the constitution for cohesion and solidarity in a modern democratic society. In this inflection, the importance of ethnic cohesion is deliberately scorned as an aspect of nineteenth-century nationalism that should be abandoned in the age of international migration.

In his recent essays, Habermas has taken a more positive stance with respect to the historical importance of the nation-state as a way of encouraging and enforcing the modernization of European societies. Moreover, now Habermas points to the democratic impulse of the nation-state: 'The

8. See Jürgen Habermas, *The Past as Future*, trans. and ed. Max Pensky (Lincoln: University of Nebraska Press, 1994), 33–54.

"invention of the people's nation" (H. Schulze) had a catalyzing effect on the democratization of state power. A democratic basis for the legitimation of domination would not
have developed without national self-awareness.' In other
words, nationalism institutes different forms of social integration and thereby creates a new and powerful model of
legitimation for the state. What Habermas acknowledges in
his most recent work is the element of solidarity among
the members of the nation as a beneficial form of social
cohesion. But he also notes the potential negative aspect
of nationalism; that is, the naturalized particularism of the
nation. He objects to the assumption that the historically
evolved and in many cases rather arbitrary structure of the
nation-state has the dignity of an end in itself to which the
lives of the citizens can be sacrificed.

Habermas's more positive evaluation of nationalism remains qualified by two factors: in the German case, he insists
on the failure of ethnic nationalism, which resulted, broadly
speaking, in the Holocaust. More generally, Habermas argues that the model of the nation-state is no longer adequate
for the global problems of the late twentieth century. Neither
in terms of economic and technological developments nor in
terms of mass migration and the pressure of environmental
questions is the nation-state truly autonomous and thus able
to offer adequate solutions. Focusing on the global nature
of communication, recently accelerated still further by electronic media, Habermas suggests that we are dealing with
a radically changed structure of the public sphere, which
can no longer be contained within national boundaries. Yet
under these conditions, the feasibility of a common democratic consciousness cannot be taken for granted. Referring
to J. M. Guéhenno, Habermas raises the question whether we

have actually reached the end of democracy. Conceding that the odds are not altogether good, he nevertheless returns to the idea of radical democracy within a larger European community. The goal that Habermas envisions is clearly not the administrative unification of Brussels but the extension of Strasbourg as a counterweight to the narrow and ultimately destructive definition of national self-interest.

In these ideas and suggestions, the utopian moments of Habermas's thought come to the fore. For him the tension between ideal and reality, respectively the normative and the descriptive level of his theory, has always been a defining element – an element that has also determined his political writings. It has marked the rhetoric of his interventions even in the case of his more incidental statements. Since Habermas is quite conscious of this aspect of his thought, he has made it part of his systematic reflection. Thus theory and praxis are dialectically linked. For this reason, the essays collected in this volume return again and again to two topics: first, the legitimation and goal of philosophy – specifically, the philosophical legitimation of political procedures and decisions; and second, the issue of language and communication. Both of these topics are tied up with the search for the possibility of universals (norms, values, morality). Here it is interesting to observe how consistently Habermas attempts to link his essays with his systematic theoretical writings.

When Habermas raises the question of philosophy he does this very much in the tradition of Critical Theory; for instance, in the tradition of Horkheimer's famous 1937 essay on the distinction between conventional and critical theory or Adorno's 1962 essay on the feasibility of systematic philosophy in the age of advanced capitalism.[9] Whereas the late Adorno felt that the tradition of systematic philosophy had come to an end and therefore favored the essay form as the most appropriate vehicle for creative thought, Habermas has never shared this radical critique of philosophy and, in particular, of rationalism. In certain ways he has remained closer to the early program of the Frankfurt School, although the epistemological and the political differences are impossible to overlook. For one thing, Habermas sees himself beyond a type of philosophy that his teachers still represented: the assumption that philosophy is charged with the task of *Totalitätserkenntnis*, the search for absolute truth, whether in the form of an ontology or in the mode of negative dialectics. By moving closer to the English and American tradition, Habermas also wants to move philosophy closer to the marketplace, thereby involving it in the issues of the day. He obviously feels comfortable with this streak of pragmatism that is so clearly at odds with the tradition of Critical Theory and most of all with Adorno's conception of negative dialectics. The pragmatic gesture notwithstanding, Habermas's defense of philosophy remains faithful to the concept of reason and rationality developed by the Frankfurt School. Thus for him the critique of rationalism and its consequences in the modern world (Max Weber) must be based on reason (*Vernunft*), specifically in the form of intersubjective communication and consensus. As much as Habermas's conception of language (as the ultimate ground of subjectivity) differs from that of Adorno, it retains the belief that reason has

9. Max Horkheimer, 'Traditional and Critical Theory,' in Horkheimer, *Critical Theory: Selected Essays* (New York: Seabury Press, 1972), 188–243; Theodor W. Adorno, 'Wozu noch Philosophie,' in Adorno, *Gesammelte Werke* (Frankfurt am Main: Suhrkamp, 1977), 10.2:459–73.

a critical potential and cannot be reduced to a mere instrumental use. Thus Habermas shows no inclination to give up on 'Occidental rationalism' and convert to cultural particularism.

This means that Habermas's understanding of legal and political issues is driven by universal claims as the ultimate horizon of theoretical reflection. Nevertheless, it is important to distinguish between abstract ideals that are seen as counterfactual and ideal situations that are already implied in everyday praxis. The 'Conversation about Questions of Political Theory' (a dialogue between him and Mikael Carleheden and Rene Gabriels) emphasizes this difference:

> For it cannot be the philosopher who – in the name of his normative theory and with the gesture of an impotent Ought – furthers a postconventional consciousness, thus sinning against a human nature that pessimistic anthropology has always led into battle against the intellectuals' dream dances. All we do is reconstruct the Ought that has immigrated into praxis itself, and we only need to observe that in positive law and the democratic constitutional state, that is, in the existing practices themselves, principles are embodied that depend on a postconventional grounding, and to that extent are tailored to the public consciousness of a liberal political culture.

According to Habermas, the tension between the actual cultural and political conditions and the implied *ought* contains the motivation for change. Pressured by his interlocutors to provide a more precise definition of the kind of 'idealization' that occurs in the ideal speech community, Habermas differentiates his own position from hermeneutic idealism as well as the positions of Apel and Peirce. The notion of an 'ideal speech situation' is treated as a strictly methodological concept. From the point of view of practical politics, such a disagreement may seem to be purely academic. For Habermas, however, it is crucial, because it determines the meaning of democracy. Democratic procedures deserve to be called democratic only when they are also reasonable; that is, based on arguments that have been tested in the public sphere. In other words, the rule of the majority as such is not a guaranty of democracy. For this reason the procedural mechanisms must be grounded in a public sphere where equal access is guaranteed to all citizens, a condition that existing democratic societies do not fulfill and that can be seen as a rigorous norm at best.

Thus Habermas's conception of radical democracy has several prerequisites: a functioning public sphere to which every citizen has equal access; the development of rational procedures for the attainment of policies and fair decisions; and finally a global dimension, that is, the fact that contemporary societies increasingly interact and thereby interpenetrate each other. Its most practical application would be the relationship between the rights of citizens and basic human rights that also protect those individuals who are not citizens. Habermas's strong feelings about the question of asylum in Germany – a constitutional right that the Kohl government decided to restrict to stem the tide of applicants for asylum [10] – are closely linked to this fundamental issue. Democracy has a global aspect that cannot be denied without negative consequences for the basic rights of the citizens. Because of their universal character, basic human rights transcend the level of the positive law as it is constituted and guarded by individual democratic societies. Also,

10. For an extensive discussion, see the essays by Manuchehr Sanadjian, Michelle Mattson, and Allison Lewis in the special issue of *New German Critique* 64 (winter 1995).

for Habermas they are more fundamental than positive laws and therefore not at the disposal of the lawmakers: 'Regarded normatively, the political legislative power is not permitted – in Germany or elsewhere – to limit or abolish basic rights.'

The question of basic human rights and their link to positive constitutional law and thereby to the sovereignty of the people represents one aspect Habermas's political theory; the other aspect is the relationship between the intercommunicative and language-oriented lifeworld and the realm of the systems driven by symbolic media such as money and power. In their dialogue with Habermas, Carleheden and Gabriels mean to detect a shift in Habermas's position, namely, a de-emphasis on the conflict between lifeworld and system. They feel that his latest book, *Between Facts and Norms*, has given up the thesis that state and economy threaten to 'colonize' the lifeworld and thereby impede democratic politics.[11] Habermas, however, insists on the basic continuity of his theory and underlines the importance of the public sphere and civil society in general as the ground for political action for which the systems have no need.

Related to this question is Habermas's concern that political decisions, which ought to be debated in parliament, are, at least in Germany, shifted to the legal system when a political deadlock has occurred or the minority is dissatisfied with the result of a vote. Clearly Habermas wants to keep basic political decisions, for instance the question of abortion rights, in the political sphere proper. He argues that the German Supreme Court (*Bundesverfassungsgericht*) should be invoked only in order to settle procedural ques-

11. Habermas, *Between Facts and Norms: Contributions to a Discourse of Law and Society* (Cambridge: MIT Press, 1996); the original German edition appeared in 1992.

tions. It is interesting to note that he is prepared to extend this understanding of radical democracy to the level of the European Community as well, at this point certainly a utopian idea for which the majority of the European nations are unprepared. In order to argue for a European democracy and against the growing criticism in England and the Scandinavian countries (as well as in Germany itself), Habermas must distinguish between the bureaucratic level of unification in Brussels (the level of the systems) and the level of actual political participation in a common European parliament in Strassbourg (the level of the lifeworld). The argument against Brussels becomes an argument against colonization that Habermas would support. The argument against Strassbourg would be an argument for national particularism to which Habermas cannot be sympathetic unless it can invoke the violation of fundamental human rights or the destruction of a political public sphere that enables the very formation of the procedures indispensable for democracy itself.

As diverse as the essays are, ranging in their topics from specifically German issues (the German past, changes in the German Republic after 1989, the tension between East and West Germany) to the assessment of intellectual trends and theoretical problems, they are written with the author's more systematic work in mind. They mediate between concrete historical situations and more general theoretical claims. For this reason they differ from Adorno's essays, which are by definition antisystematic and subversive. Habermas's conception of the intellectual, while it rejects the claim for leadership and exclusive knowledge, holds on to a paradigm of rational pedagogy. As the essays and interviews demonstrate, this paradigm is not to be confused with dry instruction based on a deductive method. Typically, their procedure is one of dialogue or of immanent criticism. They develop their force as interventions within specific social and cultural situations. For this reason – and this will be of value to the American reader – they also provide a running commentary on the history of post-Wall Germany and its relevance for the larger European context.

A BERLIN REPUBLIC

Preface by Jürgen Habermas

Incertitudes allemandes – once again the trace of German uncertainties pervades the politics and the public sphere of reunified Germany, from the Gulf War[1] and the asylum debate[2] to what to do about Stasi collaborators and the fortieth anniversary of the Nazi surrender. What we lack is an intellectual definition of clear alternatives. At the end of this volume, a discussion of the sharp break with the past made in 1945 and the 'normality' of a future Berlin Republic brings together subjects that have been the focus of my political activities over the past several years.[3]

Starnberg, March 1995

1. Jürgen Habermas, 'Ein Plädoyer für Zurückhaltung, aber nicht gegenüber Israel,' *Die Zeit*, 8 February 1991.

2. Jürgen Habermas, 'Die zweite Lebenslüge der Bundesrepublik,' *Die Zeit*, 11 December 1992; 'Die Festung Europa und das neue Deutschland,' *Die Zeit*, 28 May 1993.

3. Jürgen Habermas, *Vergangenheit als Zukunft*, Zurich, 1993.

1. Can We Learn from History?

IN AN ARTICLE in the *Frankfurter Allgemeine Zeitung* for 27 December 1993, Michael Stürmer repeated a question that has preoccupied the former Federal Republic of Germany since the 1970s, and since 1989 has succeeded in getting the new Germany's 'elite nationalists' – from Schäuble to Heitmann – really into high gear: 'Confronted by an increasing lack of grounding, however, we must ask how long the petrified guest from the past should be permitted to veto civic virtue and love of the fatherland, both in the future and in the past?' The warning about the stone guest is to be interpreted as follows: in order to become a normal nation, we should avoid self-critically recalling Auschwitz. The historian, who nonetheless himself appears in the role of history teacher, clearly regards the impulse to learn from history as a curse.

This goal, however, is not so easy to achieve as it may seem. Can we in fact learn from history? Before I offer an answer, allow me a retrospective glance, for we are not the first to ask ourselves this question.

I

Twenty-five years ago, Reinhart Koselleck took up the ancient topos of history as 'teacher' and subjected it to an in-

'Aus der Geschichte lernen?' *Sinn und Form* 2 (1994): 184–89. Text of a lecture prepared for a meeting of the Evangelical Academy in Wittenberg, organized by Friedrich Schorlemmer in January 1994.

structive historical critique.[1] The 'history' that makes its appearance in the old formula Historia Magistra Vitae did not mean to the ancients what it means to us today. For them, it did not yet refer to the whole of the historical life-context – that is, history in the singular – but rather to the rise and fall of particular histories, in which some event might serve later generations as an example for their own behavior. The Latin formula goes back to Cicero, and for Machiavelli or Montaigne history still represented a source of exemplary events. Only from the anthropologist's point of view, in which the behavior of past and present generations is seen as *similar,* can history appear as such a treasury of examples worth handing down and imitating. One can learn only from a history that repeats itself, and only those who remain similar in nature can learn from it. The topos Historia Magistra Vitae retains its persuasive force only up to the point where the historical sense of the unique and the new displaces the anthropological sense of the recurrent in the midst of change.

Koselleck shows that history's classical role as teacher comes to an end with the development of historical consciousness at the end of the eighteenth century. True, he himself draws this lesson from historical observation, and he can avoid a performative self-contradiction solely because from this point on 'history's usefulness for life' is not forthrightly denied but simply differently interpreted. It is no longer sought in traditional wisdom's recipes for dealing with typical problems, but rather in educated enlightenment regarding one's own particular, historically embedded situation, which is illuminated by both the past and the future.

1. 'Historia Magistra Vitae,' in *Vergangene Zukunft* (Frankfurt am Main: 1979), 38–66.

History as enlightenment and as historical self-understanding can, however, have quite different meanings.

The term *philosophy of history* takes seriously Schiller's conception of world history as the world court of judgment, retrospectively deciphering the cruelly ironic cunning of reason, which realizes its goals behind the backs of unconsciously acting human beings. Whereas Hegel drew from this way of regarding history the fatalistic lesson that learning always comes too late for those who act, Marx wanted philosophy of history itself to serve future generations as a lesson. The recognition of the naturally developing course of previous history is supposed to lead later generations to the insight that in the future they can free themselves to become the subjects of their own history – that is, they can make themselves into authors who produce their history voluntarily and consciously, even if not under circumstances of their own choosing. Here the historical consciousness merges with a utopian consciousness that stretches beyond the limits of the possibility of making history.

From the outset, the kind of philosophy of history that conceives the past only in relation to the horizon of its own vision of the future was criticized by the German school of historiography. The latter opposed to this 'actualism' an entirely different, historical consciousness. Ranke denied history the role of judging the past and teaching contemporaries in order to benefit future generations. For Ranke, the new disciplines then emerging were to represent earlier periods and forms of life as they really were, by means of an objectivizing assessment. The historically developed life-context of peoples was characterized by flowering and decline, but not by progress. Hence, historical understanding cannot and should not lead to practical results. Yet the contemplative imagination of what is not contemporary also retains an indirect relation to practice, insofar as the historically educated mind learns to recognize its own world in the mirror of alien worlds – that is, to recognize itself in others. Historicism is clearly always in danger of granting to a past that has been locked up in a museum, and aesthetically shaped, a crippling dominance over a present condemned to passivity. Nietzsche argued against this kind of appreciative history in the second book of his *Untimely Observations*.

Historicism robs a scientifically sterilized tradition of the vitality of *creative* power. Hermeneutics arose out of mistrust for such an anesthetizing 'experiencing,' which stands in the same relation to Dilthey as Marx stands to Hegel. Gadamer denied historical knowledge the character of simple retrospective contemplation, just as Dilthey denied it to philosophy of history. To be sure, historians' understanding is always already superseded by the context of a tradition that determines the hermeneutic starting point and thus also the historian's fore-understanding. But for that very reason, the continuation of the acquired tradition is realized through historical understanding. From this point of view the historical event gains a kernel of validity that precedes all reflection. A tradition draws its binding force above all from the spiritual authority of works that claim classical standing, against the maelstrom of criticism and forgetting; a classic is that from which later generations can still learn. It is true that this definition of the classical comes suspiciously close to tautology. Who can assure us that canon-building is done in the proper way, that what is considered classical is not simply what certain people call 'classical'? Marx's work was slow to win classical status – and quick to lose it again, after his name was taken over by a party and linked with implausible classics such as Engels and Lenin, and even Stalin.

Another tautology slips in when the sense of our initial question is altered by sleight of hand: hermeneutics is less concerned that we learn from historical *events* themselves than that we learn from texts – from traditional and dogmatically authorized teachings. I will return to this point in a moment.

II

The three modern ways of reading that I have mentioned should not obscure the fact that the traditional understanding of history as teacher has not entirely gone out of fashion. Consider the elections for the Volkskammer [People's Chamber, the ex-GDR's parliament] in spring 1990. Politicians flew in from the West and talked the population into believing that all they needed do was imitate the currency reform of 1948 in order to transform the devastated GDR into a 'blossoming landscape.' In support of this propaganda, Klein (then a government spokesman) also had prepared for the enlightenment of the GDR population advertising spots featuring pictures of Ludwig Erhard and his dachshund. Historia Magistra Vitae – the new citizens were supposed to learn from the successful history of the Federal Republic.

However, even modern readings of this topos no longer suffice to convince us that we can learn anything at all from history. Philosophy of history clearly finds a little too much rationality in history – and historicism too little. The former counts on too much room for action, the latter too little. Both – whether forthrightly oriented toward the future or attached to the past – believe historical education can illuminate the situation. In one case we are to be instructed by the voice of reason, in the other by the comparison of our life with the lives of others. And the old conception of history as teacher certainly no longer focuses on many individual stories but rather on a historically interrelated life-context. 'History' in the singular remains a source of worthwhile knowledge, however, because occasionally we still seem able to derive norms and values from it. Ultimately, hermeneutics projects this exemplary force onto a classical legacy; this anonymous event takes over and confirms itself in later generations' interpretations of it. All three versions thus share the remarkable premise that we can learn from history only when it has something positive to say to us – when it offers us a model worth imitating. That is remarkable because normally we learn from *negative* experiences, even from disappointments. Disappointments are what we seek to avoid in the future. That is no less valid for the collective destinies of peoples than for individual life histories – and for their childhood patterns.

In any event, the hermeneutic justification of history as wise teacher has on the face of it something convincing for philosophers and writers, for intellectuals, and for people working in the human sciences. We do in fact learn from our traditions, and all our lives conduct conversations with texts and minds that have remained contemporary despite their historical distance from us. As long as the substance of what Kant and Hegel said and wrote has not been exhausted, we will remain their students. The same holds for all traditions that have formed us and keep proving themselves anew so that they are continued by succeeding generations.

On the other hand, the suggestive image of the mentor role of a tradition worth knowing about is not even at issue when we ask ourselves whether and how we can learn from history. We talk not about the way a tradition silently shapes our mentality or about cultural conditioning and socialization, but about learning processes. These processes are triggered by our experiences, by the problems we encounter, and on which we frequently shipwreck with painful consequences. In unobtrusive ways, we are constantly learning from major traditions, but the question is whether we can also learn from *events* that reflect the failure of traditions. I refer particularly to situations in which the people involved find that their acquired approaches, interpretations, and abilities are not up to dealing with the problems that confront them; disappointing situations in which horizons of expectations – and even the traditions themselves that stabilize expectations – are thrown into crisis. If history plays a didactic role at all, it is as a critical authority that informs us that what our cultural legacy had up to that point considered valid is no longer tenable. Then history functions as an authority that demands not so much imitation as revision.

The year 1945 was such an eye-opening juncture for my generation. Retrospectively it revealed the rise, fall, and crimes of the Nazi regime; more precisely, it allowed us to see these as composing a chain of critical events that made evident the disturbing and disastrous failure of a population that was highly developed culturally. At the very least, that year challenged German intellectuals to conduct a scrupulous examination of a failed tradition. We had to get clear about the selectivity of a peculiarly muted history of effects (*Wirkungsgeschichte*). This history had presented us with Kant but not Moses Mendelsohn, Novalis but not Heine, Hegel without Marx, C. G. Jung without Freud, Heidegger without Cassirer, Carl Schmitt without Hermann Heller; it had left us with a philosophy without a Viennese or a Frankfurt School, legal studies without legal positivism, a psychology without psychoanalysis; it had conflated Jakob Böhme, Hamann, Baader, Schelling, and Nietzsche in order to erect a puppet-like, anti-Western, 'German' philosophy.

What became once and for all problematic that year did not, of course, concern intellectuals alone. The irrational subterranean stream of the German tradition that had risen to the surface had already caught up many people in 1914 and mobilized them against the 'ideas of 1789'; it had done away with the constitutional bases of a democratic and legal state, treating them as monstrous fruits of mechanistic thinking; it had given old anti-Semitic stereotypes a racial twist and made them acceptable among the educated middle classes and in their mandarin culture. Anyone who today questions – as did the chair of the strongest faction in the Bundestag – the legal separation of the army from the police, anyone who stokes antiforeign resentments – as the general secretary of the CDU, now the Bavarian minister president, did – verges on traditions of that kind; and he must know that he is appealing to traditions that have already failed before the critical authority of history. And anyone who would like to get rid of this authority itself by describing it as a 'petrified guest from the past' shows only that he does not want to learn from history.

Certainly, it is from the perspective of a specific generation that 1945 appears in this way as a challenging break. From other perspectives, other dates appear just as decisive. The year 1989 is a break that also opened even the blindest eyes to the rise, fall, and crimes of the Soviet Union – a chain of events that is instructive concerning the failure of an unprecedented, and unprecedentedly irresponsible, human experiment. Still written in the stars is the date that – one day – may mark the shipwreck of another regime exercised anonymously throughout the world market. The economic order that has been developed since the end of World War II does not even seem capable of controlling growing unemployment or homelessness, not to mention at least keeping within bounds the growing disparity between the generally affluent countries and the rest of the world, which is impoverished and getting poorer still.

Can we learn from history? That is one of those questions to which there exist no theoretically satisfying answers. History may at best be a critical teacher who tells us how we ought *not* to do things. Of course, it can advise us in this way only if we admit to ourselves that we have failed. In order to learn from history, we must not allow ourselves to push unsolved problems aside or repress them; we must remain open to critical experiences – otherwise we will not even perceive historical events as counter-evidence, as proofs of shattered expectations. The process of German reunification offers examples of such counter-evidence; examples of another kind are right-wing violence or ethnic conflicts in the former Yugoslavia and elsewhere, as well as the Gulf War and the intervention in Somalia. If we try to learn from such disappointments, we keep coming up against a now questionable background of disappointed expectations. Such a background is constantly being constructed from traditions, life-forms, and practices we share as members of a nation, a state, or a culture – from traditions that unsolved problems have suddenly aroused and challenged. Michael Stürmer's appeal to the unquestioned possession of civic virtues and love of the fatherland is on the contrary the surest way of immunizing oneself against the teachings of history.

2. A Double Past

What Does 'Working Off the Past' Mean Today?

I

IN 1959 THEODOR ADORNO gave a now famous lecture entitled 'What Does "Working Off the Past" Mean?' In the interim, this expression has come into common usage. Freud had talked about 'working through' and 'making conscious.' In this psychoanalytic perspective, Adorno took up a question that has recently become relevant once again: 'In trying to enlighten the public, to what extent should one delve into the past – or does emphasis on the past merely arouse stubborn opposition and thus prove counterproductive?' At the time, Adorno believed that 'what is conscious could never be as fateful as what is unconscious, semiconscious, or preconscious. It comes down to how the past is made present – whether one stops at mere accusation or stands up to the horror, through one's power to comprehend even the incomprehensible. . . . Whatever is done propagandistically remains ambiguous.' Adorno's reply is ambivalent. On one hand, he insists on mercilessly reflecting on a humiliating past that confronts us with a self different than the one we would like to be and think we are. On the other hand, this reflection can have a healing effect only if it is not used as an outside weapon against us, but becomes effective as self-reflection from the inside: 'What is done propagandistically

'Was bedeutet "Aufarbeitung der Vergangenheit" heute?' *Die Zeit,* 3 April 1992.

remains ambiguous.' This dialectical reply designates the norm for assessing the present discussion.

Adorno's commitment to 'working off' our own past, however, does not represent starry-eyed trust in the dynamics of bringing-to-consciousness, but reflects solely the insight that today, under the conditions of postmetaphysical thinking, there exists no alternative to self-reflection when we seek self-understanding. The pluralism of equally justified life-forms – which themselves leave room for individualized life-plans – does not allow us to follow set models valid for everyone. Aristotle could still point to the polis as a binding way of life that should shape the ethos of human beings. But today the success or failure of an individual life can no longer be gauged by its exemplary content, but only by the formal perspective of authenticity. It is not by chance that Kierkegaard's existential philosophy and Freud's psychoanalysis succeeded metaphysically and religiously grounded ethics. All persons must be themselves, each in his or her way. How that can be done, each person must find out by ascertaining who he or she is and would like to be. Kierkegaard's analysis of the ability to be oneself stresses temporalization; Freud's analysis of unconscious motives stresses enlightenment. A coherent and truthful self-interpretation is supposed to make it possible for us to critically appropriate and take responsibility for our own life-history. This also requires that we critique the self-deceptions we use to conceal from ourselves morally objectionable wishes and ways of behavior. The life plan and the image of the person whom we would like others to acknowledge us to be ought not to violate behavioral expectations that are just as much in the general interest. That is why in this special experience of the self, moral judgments intersect with a changed ethical self-understanding.

Such problems of course do not arise exclusively from the first person singular perspective in which we seek to explain our individual existence; they also arise in relation to an ethical-political self-understanding we as citizens of a community undertake from the perspective of the first person plural – especially when this community is burdened with a politically criminal past. It is one thing to conduct an unbiased historical investigation into the facts and causes of a failed political development; it is quite another critically to 'work off' one's own history from the point of view of the generations involved in it. In the perspective of those involved it is a matter of identity, of the articulation of an honest collective self-understanding that simultaneously suffices as a norm for political justice and expresses the deeper aspirations of a political community shaped by its history. The less repressive living conditions permit equal rights and dignified communality internally, and the more such repression was previously maintained externally by the usurpation and destruction of foreign life, the more dubious are the continuities of the traditions that determine the identity of the community, and the greater the inherited burden of a conscientiously differentiated acquisition of these traditions. Yet traditions are not freely at anyone's disposal; on the contrary, they are common property. That is why the only way the traditions can be altered is through the medium of public debate concerning the correct interpretation, case by case.

Publicly conducted ethical-political self-understanding is the central – although only one – dimension of what Adorno called 'working off the past.' It can branch out into journalism and the mass media, into school and adult-education pedagogy, into the scientific and literary public sphere, into citizen forums and official fact-finding commissions. But this must not be confused with the existential working through of personal guilt and the legal prosecution of punishable acts. Guilt in the moral as well as legal sense is attributed to individuals, whereas the citizens of a political community 'must answer for' its violations of human dignity, even if these violations have been legalized. To be sure, one of the mentality-shaping effects of state legal practices is the experience that the democratic state assumes its citizens to possess a postconventional moral conscience. The community of citizens as a whole can certainly expect of the individual a lesser or greater degree of self-examination; it can decide to exhaust the means of punishment more or less strictly. But participants in publicly conducted discourses outside the realm of the criminal justice system may take up only questions that can also be answered from the perspective of the first person plural. These issues have to do with political justice and collective identity, and also with the change of elites these perspectives may suggest. Insofar as it is not a question of appointments to public offices, the acts and fates of individuals in this context ought to have no more than the exemplary sense of illustrating typical entanglements. Moral *ad personam* accusations made in public must also remain related to the creation of politically just conditions; their aim is not the individual's existential self-understanding and they are no substitute for court judgments that can only result from a trial conducted according to proper procedures.

Personalization and tribunalization [bringing matters before a court of law for judgment] cause public debates about self-understanding to lose their focus. Both signal an overburdening with questions that should be reserved for private accountability or for legal judgments. For the ethical-political 'working off of the past' to acquire sufficient mentality-forming power and encourage a free political culture, it has to be supplemented by juridical procedure and the assumption of a certain personal willingness to engage in existential self-testing. So working off of the past is a multidimensional undertaking that also involves a division of labor.

II

The Federal Republic opens the files of the German Democratic Republic (GDR) past with far fewer reservations than do its neighbors to the east, and this cannot be explained merely by lags in cultural and social development or differences in cultural mentality. The situation of the former GDR's population is also objectively different from that of Hungarians, Czechs, Slovaks, and Poles. In the first place, the GDR gave up its own existence as a state and must for the foreseeable future live with the asymmetries in affluence, social security, and historical experiential context between East and West Germans. For a long time, it will have to make an arrangement with the great majority of 'the unaffected': 'Only Germans born after October 1990 will be united, not only in the sense that they will have comparable opportunities in life, but also in the sense that there will be an increasing correspondence in their life situation, which includes a common outlook on the future as well as a shared historical identity' (Wolf Lepenies). On the other hand, the revelation of the Stasi [the former GDR's secret police] past brings a second past, the Nazi past, back into the foreground. Whereas the peoples east of the Oder and the Neisse have to deal with their collaboration, the Germans were the perpetrators. From the outset, the GDR's role as vanquished enemy determined its special status in the East Bloc.

This history also gives the GDR population another kind of special status within a united Germany. Because the anti-fascist figures that were used to legitimize the old GDR regime stood in the way of a far-reaching settling of accounts with the Nazi past, symptoms produced by this failure to work off the past are increasing in the Eastern part of the country – a fact that de Maiziere addressed in a convincing manner when he was inaugurated as minister-president. The asymmetrical working off of the Nazi past in the East and the West is manifested, for example, in the controversies about the memorials at Buchenwald and in the construction of the ill-fated supermarket that was to be built on the site of the former concentration camp at Ravensbrück.

However, unification has also altered the political climate in West Germany. During the so-called historians' debate that took place some three years prior to reunification, it was still possible to hold off prominent figures' attempts to 'normalize' a past that 'refuses to go away,' or bring it into an 'over-arching national historical context.' Today, hardly a single voice is raised against industrious historians who emphasize, apparently without qualms, the continuity of the Bismarck Reich, or who reckon up, on the other side of the ledger, the measures taken by National Socialism to moderate its mass crimes. 'De-Stasi-fication' is seen as a form of 'de-Nazification' and tends to foster leveling comparisons between the first and the second dictatorship, between the GDR's MfS [Ministerium für Staatssicherheit, the State Security Ministry] and the Nazi Gestapo. However, such loose talk about the 'two dictatorships' remains preferable to subtle distinctions that make the Nazi regime appear as a civilized form of power in comparison with the GDR. Liberal-conservatives are transforming themselves into German nationalists, and neoconservatives talk – as they did during the Gulf War – like right-wing extremists.

Of course, not many people yield to their need for expiation quite so transparently as Ernst Nolte, who projects onto the GDR all the horrors that long preceded its existence, and which are nevertheless supposed to justify, posthumously, its fascist opponents: 'The GDR was the older German state: older than the Federal Republic, older than the Third Reich, older even than the Weimar Republic. Of course, not as a visible reality. But the GDR was the state Lenin was dreaming of when right after his October revolution he incited German workers to rise up against the blood-stained ruling classes; it was the state that might have emerged when several hundred thousand people demonstrated in January 1919 against the weak Ebert government, and were prepared to follow Karl Liebknecht's call to overthrow it; it was the state Trotzky envisioned in 1923 when he ordered Red Army generals to advise the commanders of German revolutionary troops; it was the state that Stalin was convinced had to come into existence in 1933 once the short-lived victory of Hitler's fascism had led to the inevitable collapse. But the GDR was also the state that Hitler feared when he continually referred, in his early speeches, to the "bloody swamp of Bolshevism," in which millions of people had perished; and it was the state those uncounted "bourgeois" organizations had in mind when they assured themselves and others that at the last minute, "People's Chancellor Hitler" had saved Germany from the "abyss of Bolshevism."' Nolte begins by attributing to the 'ordinary person' the 'impression' that 'the immense apparatus of state security in the GDR was able to achieve a far more intense supervision of its population than even the Gestapo,' and then presents his own conclusion: 'There are no two ways about it: those who feared and hated the GDR long before its actual existence, were not in the wrong from the outset.'

I refer to this traumatized visionary's dreams as an extreme example of the way in which the debate about the Stasi past keeps stirring up the hermeneutic dispute about the Nazi past. It is this subtext that distinguishes the working off of the Stalinist legacy among Germans from the way this legacy has been worked off in Eastern Europe: 'In Germany the double past is executed as though it had been the same thing twice over, and people are all the more eager to make up for the opportunity missed in 1945' (Eberhard Jäckel). On the other hand, even historians like Jäckel press for a differentiated judgment. Here three observations must suffice:

1. The political criminality involved in these two cases differs not only in magnitude, but also in kind. The GDR is not responsible for a world war with fifty million victims, or for the extermination of an entire people through industrialized mass destruction. The truly Stalinist crimes on German territory were committed while the Soviet regime of occupation was still in place. Only four of the GDR's forty years coincided with the dictator's lifetime. Nonetheless, the post-Stalinist regime also committed innumerable crimes – murder and torture, shootings at the Berlin Wall, abductions, forced adoptions, prohibitions on practicing one's profession, systematic surveillance of mail and telephone, hunting down and disciplining dissenters. Political punishment was merciless. The Berlin branch of the Federal Archives [Bundesarchiv] has registered 125,000 cases of human rights

violations. Each one is one too many. At least these categories of crimes have the advantage of being easier to discuss than the completely unspeakable breach in civilization associated with the name Auschwitz – especially since most of the GDR's victims survived and were not physically annihilated, like most of the Nazi's victims.

2. The fact that the GDR regime lasted a relatively long time – forty years – lent life in post-Stalinist society a kind of normality the Nazi regime failed to acquire during the twelve years of its reign, five of which were during the war. This normalizing effect seems even to have been strengthened by the panoptic surveillance of a population that had to be walled in to prevent it from escaping. The near-total penetration of the society by several hundred thousand smiling extortionists collaborating with a by-no-means-invisible State Security apparatus apparently had a flip side. The Stasi saw itself not only as an organ of repression and social control but simultaneously as a paternalist caretaker and distributor of perks, and even as a kind of surrogate for the normal channels through which interests are articulated. These channels were forbidden a population not deemed competent to make use of them and so became even more deeply entangled in the bureaucratic net of domination than they had under the Nazis. The stereotypical postwar claim that *everyone* was a victim is actually more believable today than it was then because in fact so many people were caught in the wheels of the political power machine. The ambivalent character of post-Stalinist entanglement – which became clear in the Stolpe case, little known in the West – makes moral evaluations in the complex individual cases all the more difficult. These events make significantly greater demands on our capacity for differentiation and empathy than do Nazi crimes;

the latter, because of their enormity, were relatively easy to evaluate.

3. The Nazi regime and the GDR regime also differ with respect to their intellectual foundations. To be sure, Marxism-Leninism served from the outset to legitimize an inhumane praxis. Yet even this dogmatically petrified and degenerate way of interpreting the Marxist tradition contained a critical potential that dissidents – right up to and including the Citizens' Rights movement – were able to use repeatedly against totalitarian praxis. The GDR's ambiguous and inherently fractured basis of legitimation aroused in each new generation a deceptive hope for the democratization of a system that was incapable of learning, and in so doing crippled the internal opposition. We still lack a satisfactory explanation for the peculiar form taken by bureaucratic socialism's self-elimination [Selbstabschaffung] and the intelligentsia's self-emasculation. The thesis currently asserted by a number of dissidents – namely, that the system had produced from within itself a 'counter-society' – would suggest a potential of self-criticism even in Leninistically corrupted Marxism. There is no counterpart to this in the muddled Nazi ideology. Even Wolf Lepenies does not believe that 'the end of the pseudosocialist GDR and the fall of almost all state-socialist regimes have done away once and for all with the utopian-humanitarian motives that also played a role during the growth of socialism in the nineteenth century.'

III

Considering these differences, Jäckel is right to say that it is 'foolish' to try to conduct de-Stasification on the model of de-Nazification. The initial situations in 1945 and 1989 have not much more in common than the fortunate end of a dictatorship. The end of the Nazi regime was sealed from the outside by a military defeat, the end of the GDR made possible by Gorbachev's policies and made inevitable from the inside. After 1945, the victors created a military tribunal that condemned the Nazi bigshots for war crimes and crimes against humanity – high functionaries, leading officials, generals, concentration camp doctors, and so on. Faced with these crimes, the court was able to appeal to international law and to supralegal justice. Today the internal legal system of the Federal Republic, by dint of its unification treaty, has simply been extended to the territory of the GDR. Because of the prohibition on retroactive prosecutions, the courts may only prosecute crimes that are punishable under GDR laws that were in effect during the GDR's existence (insofar as these laws themselves did not violate the principles of a legally constituted state and have not been rescinded in the interim). As in Hungary, cases that for political reasons were not pursued earlier cannot easily be prosecuted now.

Unlike 1945, there are today no spectacular cases to start off criminal prosecutions. Trials for shooting people at the Berlin Wall are directed against border policemen; even the election fraud case failed to bring one of the main culprits to trial. Whereas the de-Nazification process in 1945 caught the party small fry and minor functionaries in its far-flung net, but then let them off as fellow travelers, today the justice system is creating the deceptive impression that it is hanging the small fry and letting the big shots off the hook.

What is chiefly different is the political milieu and the overall mood. After 1945, dimly aware that Hitler had enjoyed a broad base of support, the nation held together against the 'justice of the victors,' and did so without giving a serious account to itself of the extraordinary extent of the crimes. Not long ago, Ernst Klee revealed horrifying details about the kind of help even bishops and cardinals afforded by-no-means-remorseful desk-jockeys and mass murderers. This stands in stark contrast to the current readiness to confront seriously the GDR past. The discussion of Nazi-crimes – no matter how long it took to get going – has ultimately made the 80 percent of the German population that lives in the West sensitive to the theme of coping with the past, and this time they do not have to feel themselves directly involved. In the eastern part of the country, victims and emigrants [i.e., those who fled or moved to the West during the existence of the GDR] are making sure that their fates are not forgotten. Even the editorialists of the *Frankfurter Allgemeine Zeitung* – a newspaper that for decades had nothing but scorn for the diagnosis of 'an inability to mourn' and the demand that we 'work off the past' – mirror a consensus that liberal representatives of the state, such as the federal president and the president of the Bundestag, are able to express more convincingly. For example, Fritz Ullrich Fack, who was still using very different words in speaking about 'Bitburg,' opines, 'Many people would like to repeat what was considered appropriate at that time, but which subsequently led to two generations of embittered questions, accusations, and trials: to put the files about the crimes permanently under lock and key and thus to close the painful subject of "State Security." But anyone who thinks that is possible is fooling himself.'

So today there exists a comparably advantageous starting point for the 'working off' of the second German past. This holds for all three of its aims: for changing the politically compromised elites; for the creation of political justice; and for shaping a democratic political consciousness.

Whereas an ineffective de-Nazification process could not prevent the nearly unbroken personal continuity of the Adenauer regime with the Nazi period, the liquidation and examination proceedings the West is currently forcing on the East are producing change in elites in public spheres such as politics, administration, justice, education, the universities, and so forth. Whereas it took more than a decade and a half for German justice to decide to deal with even the most obvious concentration camp crimes, the prosecutors took quick action this time, even though the facts are generally far more complicated. Legal grounds were also quickly created for civil actions leading to rehabilitation, indemnification, and restitution. Widespread complaints about the slow pace of justice have to do with the limited capacities of the investigative offices and delays caused by rather technical legal issues. But the announced political will to work legally through the injustice, which was lacking in the early Federal Republic, is credible today. The antifascist voices of liberal writers and professors (such as Karl Jaspers and Eugen Kogon, the 47 Group) got nowhere in the restorational climate of the 1950s against the deep-seated dispositions from which the Nazi-regime had already drawn its support. Today an emotionally conducted Stasi discussion – Wolf Biermann's self-portrait in *Der Spiegel* is not atypical – enters every living room.

Of course, there are also attempts to put on the brakes, and warnings are given. But the conditions for ethical-political self-understanding are more propitious than after 1945. Naturally, the problematic aspects of this process, which is as essential and desired as it is wearisome and difficult, may also appear under these conditions. Because today – in contrast to the Adenauer period – the judicial and social 'working off' process is recognized in principle by all sides, and has in fact begun, we have an opportunity to learn from the false notes and jarring practices what we can expect from the medium of public communication – and what not.

IV

The goal of *political* justice must first be achieved by means of criminal law and civil restitution. In accordance with legal principles, the criminal justice system must act regardless of the person involved; and by and large this is possible because the GDR constitution is so worded as to guarantee the essential basic rights and because GDR law not only dealt with murder and manslaughter, abduction, blackmail, and coercion, but also breaches of domestic peace, calumny, violation of the secrecy of the mails, perjury, property damage, even election fraud, and most of the other legal grounds for actions that exist in other legally constituted states. The loud demands that the justice system go after the bigwigs often conceal only a need for relief and revenge. Friedrich Schorlemmer is disturbed by 'the occasional massive appearance of the revenge mentality, which once again expects the state to do what the individual refuses to do. There are numerous anonymous denunciations and expectations that others should finally "clean out the Reds." Yesterday's gentlemen, now prostrate, are supposed to get a good working over as well. The revenge posture is a variation on that forty-year-old cowardice people are afraid to face.'

Because it lays claim to the coercive tools of the state apparatus, the course of justice must of course be conducted within well-circumscribed limits. The judges' decision-processes have to bracket out existential questions concerning personal conduct as well as moral questions concerning political responsibility, even when these penetrate the realm of political justice. This leaves open questions that must be discussed outside the realm of criminal law, in the soft medium of public dialogue, but without allowing this criticism to degenerate into show trials or entertainment.

The GDR Citizens' Rights activists around Schorlemmer, Thierse, and Ullmann first wanted to set up a sort of 'tribunal,' 'in order at least to make moral findings when judicial ability to cope with the case reaches its limits.' They had in mind cathartic conversations between perpetrators and victims in the presence of impartially judging experts. However, the dangers of *tribunalization* for the 'working-off' debate started to become more distinct during their search for 'strict forms of conversation about the elementary connection between a system and the behavior of the people who – in a variety of ways, and with differing responsibilities – had helped the system to function.' The 'public forums for enlightenment' that this group now wants to initiate throughout the country are now free of trial-like procedures and state authorization. The forums are conceived as deformalized events that avoid the misunderstanding closely connected with the trial metaphor, as if such 'tribunals' could be anything other than public relations strategy. Supralegal demands for political justice – like all contributions to ethical-political self-understanding – can become effective only through the often chaotic process of shaping public opinion and public will. They cannot be dressed-up with the aura of state authority and pushed through by means of institutionalized trials. Intellectuals who, like the Citizens' Rights activists, have acquired unquestioned personal authority because of their lifelong political conduct, cannot (nor do they wish to) claim any privileged access to truth.

They are a part of the political public sphere and not of the legally constituted political system.

Personalization is another danger threatening a discourse disseminated by the mass-media. For example, when Frau Wollenberger tells us on live television how she deals with her husband's having spied on her for the Stasi, voyeuristic intrusions into the private sphere and confusion of political with existential questions becomes complete. To be sure, functionaries, writers, and professors who bore political responsibility in exposed positions, or who exercised journalistic influence, must critically examine what they did and said. Thus it was of public interest whether National Socialist 'Giants of the Word' *[Reichswortgewaltige]* like Heidegger or Carl Schmitt admitted the political error of their ways – to which, according to Eugen Kogon, everyone has a right – or whether they kept stubbornly looking for excuses.

But insight into a personal biography – even in cases such as these – is publicly relevant only insofar as it throws light on a typical failure under typical circumstances, or can teach us something about the mechanisms of oppression – for example, about the 'planned measures' by means of which the Stasi wanted to 'dry up' the opposition's power of resistance, as it did in Wolfgang Templin's case. The only permissible public way is to delve into the structural aspects of a social and historical context where the moral norms for politically consequential behavior have been destroyed – and to acknowledge the victims. In this sense, Schorlemmer, Ullmann, and Thierse want to reconstitute 'the norms of justice and injustice,' since 'without an explanation of motives or coercions that led people to support the SED system, everyone will remain tainted by failure, and everyone, even those deserving of recognition, will be indiscriminately discredited.'

Though their first aim is a change in the mentality of the population that might produce a liberal political culture, discourses about self-understanding keep touching on questions of political justice. This is what the social process of 'working off' a politically compromised past in which everyone was in some way entangled must focus on. Then questions of political justice take a backseat to basic ethical-political questions about formative dispositions and about the traditions of a life-form of a failed normality. In such a perspective, the issue becomes the mutual pathology rather than the need to distinguish victims and culprits from the point of view of political justice. This impulse is evident in the questions Rainer Eppelmann wants the Bundestag's Investigative Commission to clarify: 'Why did hundreds of thousands of GDR citizens, in demonstrations on 1 May and 7 October, the anniversary of the founding of the GDR, shower with adulation the people who imprisoned them for thirty years? Why were 98 percent of students who were registering for school members of the Young Pioneers or the Staatspimpfe? Why were 85 or 90 percent of the employees enrolled in the FDGB [the Freie Deutsche Gewerkschafts Bund – the Free German Labor Union, the GDR union umbrella organization] despite the fact that nearly all of them knew that it had little in common with a union? Only because they hoped to get a cheap trip every two years?' Such questions have become all the weightier in view of the fact that the SED regime enjoyed far less spontaneous popular support than did the Nazis. Schorlemmer was pursuing the same goal in creating the Leipzig 'Forum for Working Off and Renewal': 'Our concern is to work off the whole of everyday life in the GDR, because up to 95 percent of the people allowed themselves to be organized and made into ballot stuffers.'

This task requires historical knowledge. But the mills of historical investigation grind slowly. Because the self-understanding debate cannot wait for the outcome of historical research and because it nonetheless needs information to draw adequate distinctions, the investigative commission is supposed to collect the available knowledge about dictatorial power-structures, about overt and covert mechanisms of suppression, forms of political resistance, and about the fellow traveler–syndrome and apathy. It is supposed to be of service in publicly working off historical knowledge.

Right now it is an open question whether we in Germany can do justice to a multileveled working-off process. The mass media are in danger of unleashing or augmenting aggressive actions directed against vulnerable and stubbornly reacting individuals. The legitimate goal in view – replacing compromised high officials – frequently serves only as a pretext for doing business. *Super!* [a reference to *Super Illu*, a magazine specializing in business opportunities in the former East Germany] is a horrifying example of this. Working off is in danger of fizzling out in the gabbing of talk shows or the staging of show trials; the spectacular controversy surrounding Christa Wolf was a bad omen.

V

We are making obvious mistakes in a situation that nonetheless appears in every respect propitious for working off the second past. The discourses being conducted in the unlimited medium of public communication must restrain themselves to avoid losing sight of their specific questions and topics, thus squandering their problem-solving energy. It is hard to maintain the right balance between 'hawks' and 'doves' [Aufwiegler und Abwiegler], particularly in view of the horrendous asymmetries that became inevitable because of the precipitous unification of East and West.

'Doves' are at work on both sides. Many of the potentially concerned are throwing up a smoke screen and want to proceed to the well-known final accounting against which Adorno warned in 1959. Thus Wolfgang Thierse asks: 'Are we condemned to repeat the history of the Federal Republic in telescoped fashion?' But the people concerned are not only the old-boy networks, unfairly put in the spotlight or shot down, not only the clever colleagues with access to high administration information, who managed to put some incriminating material aside and are now putting the files up for sale to the highest bidder. Other accomplices, too, apparently feel threatened by the time bomb in the files: 'What is certain is that Bonn, during the negotiations on unification, expressed a noticeable interest in restricting as much as possible access to MfS [Ministerium für Staatssicherheit] files, and in their rapid destruction' (Neue Zürcher Zeitung). Some upright as well as some grumpy Leftists in the West also are 'doves,' whether on reasonable moral grounds or because of embarrassing hanky-panky in matters once covered up. The first meeting of the historical commission of the German Writers Union certainly left that impression on the journalists covering the event. Regardless of these or other motives, the strength of the doves' position is not based primarily on moral grounds: it can be supported by functionalist arguments that the critics of the 'overcoming of the past' have always had at the ready.

Kurt Biedenkopf in Dresden is only expressing overtly

what the pragmatists in Bonn think: to proceed with reconstruction, we need the economic and administrative managerial elites, just as we did earlier – for instance the 'Blockflöten,' whose organizational network the CDU thoughtlessly took over in the first free Volkskammer elections in the GDR. Looked at this way, the gravitational pull of a problematization of working off history threatens economic preparedness and efficiency, internal peace and stability. The pragmatic doves, therefore, tend to favor rather limited prosecution, and observe with concern the spread and thematic extension of the Stasi discussion: 'Demoralization' is the buzzword familiar from defensive battles in the old Federal Republic.

This interpretation, which brings the normative objectives of political justice and a consciously produced change in mentality into conflict with the functionalist imperatives of economic development and social stability, is astonishingly shortsighted. Looking back on a transfigured postwar period, it confuses two facts in particular. First, the exceptional character of the propitious situation in which continuous and widespread improvement of living conditions could be translated into 'trust in the system' among a population protected from further crises; second, the intellectual tensions and conflicts activated during the sixties, which a generation after the war helped transform that trust in the system into a liberal mentality that is politically and culturally anchored. In short, the functionalist arguments are too short-winded; the 'success story of the Federal Republic' praised forty years later would also have been impossible, had there not been far-reaching change in normative positions and had it not become accustomed to a culture that fosters opposition.

In addition to defensive 'doves' there are others who –

even if they overreact at times – certainly should not be lumped together with the 'hawks.' Had it not been for the engagement of the Citizens' Rights activists who early on took possession of the Stasi archives and kept them from being destroyed, had it not been for the Volkskammer's laborious, last-minute decision and the tough fight in the Bundestag concerning access to the files, had there been no proposal for tribunals, had the revelations – initially triggered by emigrant writers and prominent victims – not had a dynamic of their own, the opportunity for open public discussion would have remained largely unexploited, and the GDR past would have been swept under the rug of the Federal Republican victory. Some people who were deeply wounded, often to the quick, are asking for satisfaction – and deserve it. It would be shameless to call them 'hawks.' Loudly protesting against law and order is a public service, when law and order have been so corrupted, even if highly personal motives may be involved, creating the occasional impression that the accusation is connected rather with an obstructed martyr's role, or feeds on rage about the postrevolutionary impotence of those who initiated the change in the first place.

Another matter altogether is the unholy alliance between the rancor of the old anti-Communist fighters and the injured subjectivity of the victims. As if by chance, in the West's slick magazine articles many such issues were nonetheless conflated, for technical reasons, because the former GDR had not had time to develop its own public sphere with its own infrastructure and discourses. That is why intellectuals in the East are frequently manipulated by journalists in the West, walking unwittingly right into the no-man's-land between the petrified front lines, which continue to reflect the political and intellectual trench warfare of the

1960s and 1970s. The cold warriors are using the Stolpe case
to renew their lost battle against engagement with the East;
in the Bundestag, the past is dealt with along party lines;
and in magazines our intellectuals 'on duty' once more re-
lieve themselves of feelings about the East Berlin academy
more suited to Günter Grass's and Walter Jens's unintimi-
dated intransigence and assumptions, which were so long
opposed. This way of heating up the debate makes the overdue working off of the past into an instrument for ends other
than political justice and a self-critical change of consciousness; it inflames the potential for mutual injury, a potential
inherent in all the self-understanding debates. Tribunalization and personalization erase the limits on such discourses,
which, although they *touch on* moral, legal, and existential questions, cannot allow themselves to be determined by
their logic, which leads to the attribution of personal guilt
and the evaluation of the way an individual has led his life.

VI

There is an additional difficulty. The enlarged Federal Republic is the wrong framework for an ethical-political self-
understanding that – for compelling internal reasons –
ought to be conducted under symmetrical conditions and
from the perspective of a mutual *we*. But for the time being
there are two unequal parties, one of which is in many respects 'evaluating' the other. The apparently magnanimous
but hasty rhetorical leveling of differences between the Eastern and Western experiential contexts – differences that will
continue to exist for a long time – leads only to false symmetries. To be sure, existing asymmetries also lead to a false
affirmation of differences: 'West Germans sometimes ap-
proach us,' Schorlemmer rightfully complains, 'as our trea-

surers as well as our judges. We East Germans have less and less to say. Hardly anyone is even *speaking* any more. Once again we are being turned into morons and foreigners in our own country.' West Germans are only too eager to assume supervision of the process by which their brothers and sisters achieve self-understanding. But this cannot be countered – as happened recently with the Bundestag's investigative commission – by appealing to false commonalities. The working-off process cannot be defined as a seamless *pan-German* enterprise.

In the climate of growing national self-confidence and demands for a new German normality; in the climate of an ahistorical, loudmouthed policy toward Croatia, cooling with regard to the idea of Europe, and the truly hysterical defense of our national symbol, the 'Deutschmark,' against the excessive foreignization involved in the adoption of the Latinate term 'ECU' to denominate the new European currency – in such a climate the appeal to the Germans' common fate comes very close to suggesting that we should turn back to the very spiritual continuities that we in the Federal Republic fended off with such great effort and, indeed, for the first time in recent German history.

The benefit of this cleansing self-reflection would be squandered, were we to turn back to that Teutonic mix of muddy and deep thoughts that once seemed to Heidegger our 'most authentic' *['Eigenste']* quality.

While the appeal to false commonalities has a regressive side, with regard to the future it also conceals an asymmetry that imposes a considerable burden on a self-understanding discourse that is not entirely domestic. The GDR's self-dissolution has shifted the axis of the political decision-making processes to a more general commonwealth, in which those who participate directly in, and are affected by, the working off of the second past represent a comparatively small minority. Unless the change in mentality is connected retrospectively with political decisions that people can regard as *their own,* important ways of measuring the success of collective self-understanding will be lacking.

We must acknowledge that the constitutionally established unification signifies that both sides have opted for a common future and a reciprocal understanding with regard to the two different postwar histories – against the background of a common, all-overshadowing Nazi era. The working off of a *double* past – made necessary by the GDR's Stalinist legacy – is for the time being possible only in a double perspective. Here Wolfgang Thierse is right: the way East Germans confront their history will decide whether the West Germans also take a further step 'in working through their own history.'

One starting point for this discussion might be the observations made by Gerd Heidenreich, the president of the West German PEN Center, in a recent interview: 'The basic question really is: what were the conditions, occasions and reasons for the seamless continuation of the Nazi Blockwart [neighborhood warden] mentality in one part of Germany? If we are honest with ourselves, we have to assume that it would also have persisted here in the West had it been encouraged and rewarded with perks. The settling of accounts with the Stasi past does not allow us to avoid inquiring into the common bases of the German states, and the historical presuppositions for a state that allows no internal contradictions.' Even this proposition might be misunderstood in a heated climate. It is surely not the thesis of a 'dove' who stresses the force of circumstances in order to exculpate retrospectively the fellow travelers of 'both dictatorships.'

Replies to Questions from a Bundestag Investigative Commission

IN THE TWO preceding hearings it was a matter of interpreting facts. The concluding discussion faces a different question: what *should* we do with the investigative commission's findings, if we want to promote a political culture that stabilizes the democratic constitutional state? If only because of that question's normative character, I am not assuming the role of an expert here, but only that of an intellectual participating in a public discussion. The commission, in this its last hearing, is entering the public process of 'working off the history of the two German dictatorships,' which is our mutual subject. The question as to the meaning of this process for the condition of democracy you have divided into four subquestions. I shall address each of these in the order in which they were presented.

How important is 'working off' the past for the stability of democratic order and its social values?

The expression 'working off the past' derives from the title of a 1959 essay in which Theodor Adorno endorsed public discussion of the Nazi period. The controversy about the advantages and disadvantages of a reflective preoccupation with this past, including its dark aspects, has been with us ever since. The opposing side fears the destabilizing effect of such

'Antworten auf Fragen einer Enquete-Kommission der Bundestags,' *Deutschland Archiv* (July 1994): 772–77. The session took place on 4 May 1994 in the Berlin Reichstag building.

a historical pedagogy; constant reflection, it is said, destabilizes the traditions that have to nourish a nation's political self-understanding; instead of making people aware of a disturbing past we should seek to mobilize pasts that can be endorsed. The publication of the Stasi documents touched off a similar controversy in 1989. I regard the oppositions between destabilization and final reckoning, between communicative silence and self-destructive moralizing as false alternatives, for the following reasons:

(a) First, I doubt that we have a choice between cover-up and self-criticism: painful experiences cannot be blocked out by a conscious act of will. To be sure, one can *decide* to declare an amnesty or to keep the files secret, but one cannot *arrange* a repression of dissonant recollections, even assuming such an arrangement would produce the desired result. Moreover, filtering out retrospectively devalued convictions and forms of behavior does not even serve to stabilize self-images, for unpleasant truths are hard to control; at any time they can rend the veil of an illusory or only uncomfortably skewed self-understanding. The history of the Federal Republic provides an example of this. In the favorable conditions obtaining in the first years after the war, something resembling an economically and socially based 'trust in the system' took root among a population safe from further crises. But it was not transformed into a loyalty to the constitution anchored in the convictions of a liberal political culture until the normative confrontation with the Nazi past began in the 1960s.

(b) Another confusing suggestion is that the political order of a *modern* community might be based on a naturally developing – and thus unquestioned – background consensus. What unites the citizens of a society through a social, cultural, and philosophical pluralism consists in the first place only in the abstract foundations and procedures of an artificial republican order that have been produced in the medium of law. Constitutional principles can take root in the citizenry only after it has had good experiences with the constitutional institutions and *become accustomed* to conditions of political freedom. In this way, citizens learn to appreciate the republic and its constitution as an achievement within their own national context. Without such a historical representation [*historische Vergegenwärtigung*] patriotic constitutional bonds cannot be forged. For example, for us these realities are connected with our pride in a successful Citizens' Rights movement, but also with the dates 1848 and 1871, with the horrors of the two world wars, with the bitterness of two dictatorships, and with anguish concerning a human catastrophe – one with an unheard-of number of victims, and from which no lesson can be extracted except that any kind of state-engineered killing must be abolished.

(c) Finally, we must keep firmly in mind that, contrary to a widespread misunderstanding, the demand for a 'working off' of this past does not require that we blindly trust in the psychological dynamics of bringing something to consciousness. Rather, it reflects the insight that we can learn only from history seen as a critical authority. History as 'teacher' is an ancient topos; but the positive ways of reading this topos lead into the wilderness – we might have learned at least that much from our frequent misuse of history.

The ancients' anthropological view of history focused on the eternal return of the invariably changing – on history as a treasure trove of exemplary events that are worth imitating. But modern authorities, whose historically honed consciousness is more interested in the particular and unique, still want to learn something positive from history. The philosophers of history sought reason in history; historicists tried to recognize what is themselves in the face of the other; hermeneuticians appealed to the power of classical models. Since then we have become skeptical with regard to the premise common to all three of these ways of reading history; namely, that we learn from history only if it tells us something positive, something worth imitating. This premise is not very persuasive, because we also learn, and more often, from negative experiences, and even from disappointments, which we seek to avoid in the future. This is true for the collective destinies of peoples no less than for the life histories of individuals. We learn historically chiefly from the way historical events challenge us, showing us that traditions fail, and that we and the convictions that heretofore guided our actions have gone aground on the problems that must be solved. Many dates in recent German history, and not only the year 1945, had this power to overthrow our convictions.

What does the legacy of the two dictatorships signify for contemporary and future German culture?

The Federal Republic not only took on the German Reich's heritage in matters of international law; it also assumed political responsibility for the consequences of the 'Third Reich.' The entry of the GDR into the Federal Republic changed nothing in this legal succession, but it did change a few things in relation to the political-historical inheritance. The weight of the Nazi past is now being overlaid with a brief Stalinist past and a longer authoritarian, post-Stalinist past.

This succession of two dictatorships offers an instructive sharpening of our perspective on their common totalitarianism and draws attention to the structural dispossession of citizens who were robbed of their social and legal autonomy. When I look over the various topics on which the investigative commission consulted with experts – the amalgamation of party and state apparatus; the organization of the state security system, which included every aspect of life; the judiciary and prosecution; the militarization of society; the methods of forced collectivization; the role of bloc parties and mass organizations; the use of the media as an instrument of domination; the reorganization of the educational system; a form of psychosocial repression that reached into everyday life, and so on – there emerges an image of a panoptic state that directly undermined not only a bureaucratically dried-up public sphere but also its foundation: the society of citizens and the private sphere. If one regards this image as negative, there arises the counter-image of a legal order affording all its citizens equal private and public autonomy, which eliminates the amalgamation of the forces of domination and erects barriers against state injustice.

However, we ought not to let our recollection of the first past grow pale by comparison with the now so starkly illuminated second one. The Nazi period bears the unmistakable stamp of an officially announced, bureaucratically executed targeting, and a comprehensive, industrialized annihilation, of an internal enemy defined by certain characteristics. This monstrous fact lets us see the normative heart of a democratic constitutional state: symmetrical conditions of recognition that assure everyone equal respect. Contrary to what Carl Schmitt and his students continue to assert (as recently as the *Frankfurter Allgemeine* for 22 April 1994), this mutual recognition should not be limited to members of a homogeneous people defending themselves against external

45

and internal enemies; it relates not to a nation of ethnically bonded countrymen, but to a nation of citizens united by the same rights. That is why the decisive lesson of 1989–90 for the citizens of the Federal Republic does not consist in the reestablishment of a nation-state, nor in the entry of compatriots in the eastern part of Germany into the civil order of a prospering society, but in the achievement of citizen rights and the elimination of a totalitarian regime.

How can knowledge about the two German dictatorships be transmitted through political education and how is it possible to maintain awareness of the threats to a free democracy?

The 'double past' makes unusually high demands on our perspicuity and ability to differentiate, on our powers of judgment, tolerance, and self-criticism. Let me remind you of four difficulties.

(a) The comparison between the two dictatorships demands – from the historians who instruct us about the differences and similarities of the two dictatorships, but also from ourselves, the citizens – a readiness to distance ourselves from our own political biases. In their effort to legitimize themselves, both regimes made use of a store of ideas that reaches back to the nineteenth century on one hand and, on the other, still holds sway over the present. The division between Left and Right, which ought not to be prematurely retired, becomes disturbingly noticeable when the two dictatorships are compared. Whereas those on the Right tend to find commonalities, those on the Left see primarily differences. The Left ought not to deceive itself about the specific common points of totalitarian regimes and must use the same yardstick in both cases; the Right should not erase or downplay the differences. I refer not only to differences arising from the contrary ideological content, from entirely different kinds of political criminality, or from the different life-spans of the two regimes and the corresponding degree of normalization of everyday living conditions; I refer also to the fact that later generations are responsible in a different way for a National Socialism that arose in our own country and was widely supported, as compared with an authoritarian socialism that was imported by conquerors and adopted by the population.

Now for the first time an antiauthoritarian consensus – one deserving of that name because it is not selective – can be formed among us. This ought to be a common basis on which Right and Left can then differentiate themselves from each other. That may be easier for the young people now taking their place in society than for us who are older. Only when political socialization does not occur under the polarizing general suspicion of internal enemies can liberal attitudes and democratic conviction do without the midwifery of anti-Communism or antifascism.

(b) A second difficulty is connected with a different aspect of the 'double past.' The real working off of GDR history is taking place against the background of a de-Nazification process that has itself become historical. On the one hand, the very different initial situations in 1945 and 1989 do not allow us to conduct de-Stasification on the model of de-Nazification; Eberhard Jäckel rightly calls this 'nonsense.' On the other hand, the criteria on which criticism is based have also changed in the interim. Whereas the kind of confrontation with Nazism that goes to the heart of the formation of mentalities was conducted only superficially in the East, and in the West only after a considerable delay, today there is a readiness to deal energetically with the issue that was neglected after 1945. The significance of the Nazi mass crimes, which was only gradually comprehended, helped sharpen our Benjaminian loser's viewpoint, seeing from below the barbarous underside of a history written by and for winners. (Incidentally, this is the case not only for us. Heightened empathy with helpless victims has also awakened ugly memories in other countries – memories of the destruction of Native American cultures, the bloody suppression of the uprising in the Vendée, the Armenian genocide, the destruction of the Kulaks, etc.) We find ourselves in a dilemma: if today – with the laudable intention of making up for the errors of a problematic 'overcoming of the past' – we use different standards than we did earlier, then historically speaking we are violating the principle of equal treatment. This paradoxical form of not entirely groundless unfairness manifests itself chiefly in the desirable change in elites in the former GDR (e.g., in the realm of higher education), which was harsh, but nonetheless carried out in a rigorous manner.

(c) A third difficulty stems from the asymmetrical distribution of the weight of the legacy. The Germans in the East and West share only the first past. Their role in the history of the GDR differs: East Germans are deeply involved both as perpetrators and as victims; at most, West Germans affected the conditions and developments in East Germany from the outside, through 'internal German' or 'binational' relationships. Naturally, the Federal Republic's Germany policy, the reaction of the West German population to the national partition and to the fate of their East German brethren, the contacts and the noncontacts between here and there, the role of the media and intellectuals, and so on, are of great interest for working off the interdependencies of the two postwar histories. But these divided pasts were also constitutive for different experiential contexts. A premature leveling out of these differences will only tempt us to make backward-directed appeals to misleading continuities of long-since questionable aspects of our tradition. If we don't want to sink back into the fetid German swamp, we must keep the very gradual civilizing process of the old Federal Republic from disappearing behind the artificially constructed symmetries of two allegedly equally dependent component states, both of which were deprived of their sovereignty.

Only if we admit the asymmetrical conditions of the inheritance in the East and the West, only if we do not define the 'working off' process as an *uninterrupted* overall German enterprise, can we avoid deluding ourselves concerning the obstacles that stand in our way. The population of the former GDR no longer commands a political public sphere of its own that is not coupled to that of the West; it is incapable of pursuing a self-understanding of its second past in its own home. This requires special tact from us in the West – those of us who, without any special effort on our own part, escaped specific entanglement in state Socialism.

(d) Up to this point we have been discussing comparative distinctions between the two dictatorships – the two working-off processes and the two postwar histories. But we must also distinguish between the normative points of view under which these past periods are judged. On one hand, an unjust regime has left behind the thirst for satisfaction, for the *reestablishment of political justice,* so far as that is possible, and on the other, the *desire for a change in the mentality of the population* that will produce and stabilize democratic conditions. The material the investigative commission has prepared is useful for both purposes, in which the objective

49

of a democratic change in mentality is supposed to be primary.

Questions of justice can be legal or moral in nature. They involve both restitution for injustices and individually accountable guilt. Legal claims and moral accusations are raised by one party against the other; these are the expression of their splitting into culprits and victims. The proceedings sought aim, of course, at producing reconciliation, insofar as the intersubjective recognition of judgments that are made in the light of valid norms is able to reconstitute a violated order. This aim of political justice is achieved mainly through criminal law and civil indemnification. However, since legal sanctions [Zwangsrecht] are for good reasons severely circumscribed in their application, many political-moral cases in which people ought to be held responsible are withdrawn and then reserved for political procedures (such as the Stolpe Commission) or for informal public discussion (e.g., the dispute between the Citizens' Rights activists or exiled writers and the representatives and collaborators of the old regime). Questions of ethical and political self-understanding raised in common by members of a collective, concerning important aspects of the way of life they all share, are of different nature. Questions other than those concerning justice, which are decided by an impartial third person – that is, questions that touch on the collective identity – require answers from the we – from the perspective of the first person plural. From this perspective we can discuss, not the individually accountable acts that separate, from the point of view of political justice, the guilty from the innocent, but rather the pathologies of a common way of life, the shaping dispositions of a failed normality of the everyday. The crucial point in the working off of a politically burdened past – for which everyone involved, even members of the opposition, is responsible – is found in such consciousness-changing processes of self-understanding. These can be stimulated but not organized.

After the commission concludes its work it should reflect on one particular threat to the political culture of the enlarged Federal Republic, which proceeds from the unintentional consequences of an unfortunate mode of state unification. Whereas the resistance against Hitler manifested on 20 July 1944 – no matter how selectively it may always have been described – was incorporated into the founding conception of the Federal Republic, the historical achievement of the Citizens' Rights movement in the GDR eludes the national consciousness. This movement might have found an appropriate symbolic representation in a republican refounding of the Federal Republic. Because a discussion of the constitution was itself anxiously avoided, the cry 'We are the people' has remained without lasting echo. That is one reason why the people in eastern Germany, feeling violated by a process of unification that in many ways deprives them of their dignity, are turning backward – and cling to old identities instead of making their own contribution to democracy a source of self-confidence.

Within what institutional framework ought further historical-political 'working off' proceed?

The mills of science grind slowly. Debates about self-understanding arise from other impulses and obey other periodicities than those of research; they cannot wait for research results and yet depend on informative and clarifying reports to keep the complexity of the topics from disappearing in the maelstrom of mass communication. That is why it was wise to create a commission to seek out and sift through the available expert knowledge and prepare it for the political public sphere. Whether this work ought to continue within a different institutional framework – thus raising the level of the discussions that will be conducted anyhow – will also depend on the quality of the results.

After 1945, the first professorships and institutes for contemporary history and political science were set up in order to investigate National Socialism with a view to political education. Similar organisms – like the Institut für Zeitgeschichte [the Munich Institute for Contemporary History] or the Zentrum zur Erforschung der SED Diktatur [the Potsdam Center for the Investigation of the SED Dictatorship] – have recently been created. Moreover, the Federal Republic now possesses a far-flung network for political education that absorbs and evaluates the relevant information. This network begins with social science instruction, academic publications and conference activities, state centers for political education and the political party foundations, and also includes exhibitions mounted by historical museums, as well as the political sections in the newspapers and magazines and TV news and talk shows. This communications network – which is very dense in comparison with that of other nations – functions on the basis of a comparatively solid formal education available to all segments of the population.

Two other points strike me as more relevant: the relationship of the working-off process to (a) historical investigation and (b) everyday politics.

(a) The historian as a writer of history is accustomed to writing for a public of educated laymen. Presentations of national history that made literary demands on the reader exerted an influence on the broadening and shaping of national consciousness, especially during the nineteenth century. The historical consciousness that began to emerge at the end of the eighteenth century became the medium for the articulation of a new national self-understanding, which was first conveyed by the academic elites and then until 1848 gripped the masses. This connection between historicism and nationalism has dissolved in the interim. Institutionalized scholarship, now embedded in specialized public spheres, obeys imperatives other than those of the public use of history for the purpose of political self-understanding. The historians' roles change accordingly. Historians leave scholarly discourse behind when they turn to the general public; and even then we have need to determine whether they are asked as experts or appear unasked as intellectuals.

In the disputes about interpretation in the political public sphere, the only participants are those who engage themselves in the light of competing value orientations, and confront each other concerning them – as they did, from about 1990 on, regarding their identity as citizens of the enlarged Federal Republic and as the heirs of this 'double past.' Insofar as we are concerned with facts and interpretations of facts, we depend on the judgment of experts who draw a core content of facts out of the controversy and decide – not only in extreme cases such as the so-called Auschwitz lie – with scholarly authority what should be regarded as true or false. But the public use of history is not *exhausted* by the digestion of facts by experts. Citizens make a different demand on history in the dispute about an authentic self-description or about the best interpretations of the origin and definition of their political community: they take from history the fundamental controversial grammars for their conceptual perspective, description, and punctuation of the course of historical events.

The controversy about how to punctuate contemporary German history has flared up anew since unification. Someone who sees the period 1914 to 1989 as a uniform era, whether as an era of ideologies, of a world civil war, or of totalitarianism, will ascribe a different status to the Nazi period than will someone who sees – from a German perspective – the period between 1871 and 1945 as a nationalistic phase, with the victorious march of the democratic constitutional state beginning only after 1945. A different interpretation will produce other ruptures and turning points. For example, anyone who accepts the claim that German history follows a 'special path,' and turns it on its head, arguing that the Federal Republic of 1945 to 1989 was a more or less pathological interim period, is free to trivialize the turning point of 1945 into an 'antifascist reformation' and, instead, to understand 1989 as the break that 'finishes off the raison d'être of old Federated States,' thus opening the way to a return to the alignments of the Bismarck Reich. But, on the other hand, whoever takes the fall of the Weimar Republic as the turning point – and has an interest in a democratic culture – will draw less hope from the re-acquired 'national state normality' of 1990 than from the level of political civilization that had by then been reached in the old Federal Republic.

There is a broad spectrum of such background theories; they even have their legitimate place in historical research. But when in public usage they turn into the crystallization points of a new collective identity, they lose their exclusively cognitive function. And historians who advance such controversial viewpoints and conceptions from the specialized public sphere of their fields, and intervene as essayists or writers of history in an identity-building process of self-understanding, are changing their roles. Then they are no longer endowed with the authority of experts but are participating as intellectuals with equal rights in the discourse of citizens.

(b) While it is important to differentiate self-understanding from science, self-understanding cannot be severed, on the other hand, from politics in general. A retrospective working off of the past receives its orientation from a contemporary horizon of future-directed interests and expectations. That is why the working off of the past is *constantly* in communication with contemporary political questions. Self-understanding cannot be related *in abstracto* to values, but always stands in a hermeneutic relationship with the understanding that is reached concerning contemporary challenges. Each corrects the other. The lessons we draw from our experiences with two dictatorships – the traditions we appropriate, and those we revise – are significant today for the questions of how we will regulate our coexistence with minorities, what kind of immigration policy we will have, what kind of Europe we should strive for, how we are going to define our interests with regard to central and eastern Europe, how we should define the new role of the UN, and how – within that framework – we want to define the role of the Bundeswehr. These options also throw new light on the past; they influence the decision as to whether we are going to engage in a 'working off' process, whatever its result may be, or instead deny from the outset that it has any point, in order that we may finally, as is repeatedly urged, shake off 'the mentality of a defeated people' and 'the metaphysics of guilt.' In this fashion our discourse about self-understanding combines, like two communicating vessels, the interpretation of our origins with our orientation toward the future.

3. German Uncertainties

French Views, French Anxieties:
An Interview with *Le Monde*

YOU DISTINGUISH YOURSELF *from your German university colleagues by engaging in controversial public debates. Your contributions also come to the attention of the international public. First of all, regarding your philosophical background: you regard the dangers to our civilization, which Adorno and Heidegger saw as an inescapable fate, more as a practical challenge.*

I would not mention Adorno and Heidegger in the same breath. Of course, both of them dramatize their diagnoses of our time by means of a comprehensive historical perspective of decline. In 'instrumental reason' or 'the framework of technology,' fateful tendencies to self-empowerment and reification are said to break through and reach back into the archaic. However, Adorno knew that even the most radical critique of reason is dependent on the power of negation, which derives from reason itself. Unlike Heidegger, he never became an opponent of Enlightenment. That is why Adorno was sufficiently inconsistent to speak and act differently as a public intellectual than one might have expected from a theoretician of the 'administered world.' Despite his theoretical pessimism, his attitude toward the general public was almost that of an adult-education teacher.

'Französische Blicke, französische Befürchtungen,' Le Monde, 13 September 1993. The interview was conducted by Roger-Pol Droit and Jacques Poulain.

*But as an intellectual don't you assume a different – more prag-
matic – position on public questions than Adorno or Heidegger did?*

Perhaps my generation was the first to free itself from certain pretensions of German mandarin culture. After the war
we made better contact with the Anglo-American spirit.
Philosophy meanwhile has gained a more clearly defined
awareness of its own fallibility. I trust neither the philosophical tradition's 'strong' concept of theory – that is, truth
with a capital T; nor do I mourn the loss of this knowledge
of totality – as does Negative Theology.

*All right, but you still would like to say what's at stake in our
time and how we can meet its challenges. What topics are you
particularly working on, and what objectives are you pursuing?*

That question can be answered with a whole book or with
one sentence: I feel that Max Weber's question regarding the
paradoxes of rationalization is still the best key to a philosophically and scientifically informed diagnosis of our time.

What does that mean?

Without undue self-commiseration we ought to get clear
about the ironic pattern of a socially and culturally self-
denying progress, and hence about the price paid for a modernization to which we continue to cling. At present a rather
undialectical critique of Enlightenment is dominant, from
which we cannot learn very much. When Adorno and Horkheimer spoke of 'instrumental reason,' they did not mean
that reason could simply be equated with a self-asserting
subject's objectivizing act of understanding. The point they
were trying to make was that a form of understanding that

has ballooned into a totality is usurping the place that properly belongs to reason. Enlightenment turns into positivistic myths, showing – especially in our century – its own barbaric flip side. The unconcealed horrors of existing unreason have eliminated the last remnant of an essentialist trust in reason. Yet so far as we can see, there still exists no alternative to a modernity that is now conscious of its own contingencies. The less we indulge in imaginary evasions, the less tempted we will be to reinterpret the risks inherent in modernism in order to make of them a *fatality* prepared long in advance. There is neither a higher nor a lower reason to which we can appeal, only a procedurally sobering reason – a reason that proceeds solely on sufficient grounds; a reason that puts itself on trial. That is what Kant meant: the critique of reason is reason's proper task.

But isn't that the old rationalism?

Not if the dialectic of enlightenment is motivated by the radically anti-Platonic mistrust of ideological consolation through false generalities. The work of self-critical reason consists in overcoming its own unreasonable projections. Such a reason can translate its critical energies into the binding powers of a noncoercive, unifying form of communication. I mean the power of intersubjective understanding, which in cases of conflict is the only alternative to the use of force. That is what – by means of the noncoercive force of the better argument – enables nonviolent agreement as well as agreement between strangers who need this kind of communication so as to acknowledge each other as strangers and to respect each other, precisely in those regards in which they are 'other' and are distinguished from each other.

To become a bit more concrete: The radical transformations in Eastern and Western Europe have fundamentally altered our era's self-understanding. Are contemporary problems still the same as the ones you identified and investigated in the 1960s and 1970s from the point of view of empancipatory activities? Or do today's problems seem to you to be of a wholly different kind?

Well, the 'remedial revolution' we witnessed with astonishment and enthusiasm can be called an emancipation. Certainly, no one had foreseen this bankruptcy of state Socialism. An unexpected event of world-historical magnitude naturally brings new problems along with it, problems we could not have dreamed of ten years ago: the retranslation of a decrepit state economy back into private capitalist relationships; the return of ethnically motivated civil wars and nationalist conflicts; the disintegration of a bipolar world order; and a new alignment of powers in central Europe. On the other hand, deep ruptures of this kind also create their own illusions: we forget that the new problems throw no new light on our old problems. They only divert attention from them.

What are you thinking of?

Statistics show that currently seventeen million people are unemployed in the European Community. The prognosis for the OECD countries in 1994 is thirty-six million unemployed. The next upswing is going to take place on the model of 'jobless growth.' That means that our societies' tendencies toward segmentation will grow – with the kind of consequences we are familiar with from the United States – ghettoization, the utter neglect of the inner cities, increased criminality, and so on. Not to speak of the problems of immigration, ecology, women's equality, and so forth. In short, the problems we addressed before 1989 from the perspectives of the social and ecological reconstruction of industrial capitalism have only become more stubborn. However, the drastically increasing interdependence of world events has deprived everyone of the illusion that we can continue to treat these matters from our nationally limited perspectives. The responsibility the West is beginning to feel for the growing misery in eastern Europe, the worldwide migration streams – whose causes cannot be eliminated without reconstructing the former Third World; the pressure of international conflicts and the new role of the UN: all that has made us more sensitive to the global dimension of the synchronicity of the dissynchronous.

Are you reckoning with an increase in insoluble crises throughout the world, or do these crises contain the germ of their own solution?

That I don't know. Some aspects of our reactions are perhaps too subjective. The perceived accumulation of worldwide problems has a crippling effect on many observers. Systems theory is disseminating a message that is finding a response again: everything is changing but nothing is working any more. I have the feeling that a situation that existed at the beginning of the European workers' movement is repeating itself; then the masses rose up against the domination of the bourgeoisie, but now it is occurring on a worldwide basis and with a different portent. However, the masses from the impoverished regions of the world lack effective sanctions against the North: they cannot go on strike; at most, they can 'threaten' with waves of immigration. And what was in Europe an unintended side effect of the push to emancipation has become a declared goal today: integration into the life-forms of the affluent societies; that is, participation in a civilization that is broadcasting its achievements globally and whose vanguard of TV series, Coca-Cola, and blue jeans has truly penetrated every last corner of the world. At the same time, we know that, if only for ecological reasons, the level of affluence that is part and parcel of this civilization cannot be transposed onto the world as a whole.

Radical transformations are striking the Federal Republic in a special situation. As compared with the states to the East, which must actively solve their problems on the basis of their regained political independence, Germany – which is in the process of reunifying – is looking itself in the face. Will it be able to deal with this introverted situation on its own?

Fortunately, as France's closest partner and as a member of the EC, we are not alone. Besides, for a country as dependent on exports as the Federal Republic, the formally reconstituted state sovereignty remains somewhat fictitious. On the other hand, if such fictions happen to give wings to the masses' – or only to the elites' – imagination, they can acquire a weight of their own. Some people are again dreaming of a renewed German superpower in Central Europe. That is why the kind of political mentality with which Germans emerge from their self-encounter matters. Many West Germans feel that in East Germany they are encountering part of their own past. This stirs up legitimate recollections and nostalgic feelings, but also unconscious motives that seemed long forgotten. Even among intellectuals, we encounter peculiar sentiments, e.g., relief that by overcoming our division as a nation we have also overcome an allegedly excessive cultural foreignization, and can now return to what is most 'our own.' Instead of letting such matters lie undisturbed, we need an open debate about the role of the new Germany. This self-understanding ought to have taken place within the framework of a constitutional debate. That was impossible because of the precipitous speed of the re-unification.

In this connection, what status do you assign to the debate about the change in the right-of-asylum law? Do you foresee the same dangers in France where the government, with its reform of the right of citizenship, has put into doubt the ius soli *that has been in force since the Revolution?*

The French minister of the interior, M. Pasqua, acted quickly after the change of governments. In the Federal Republic, great damage was done by the way the conservative parties played this subject off against a helpless opposition. Against the background of the previously mentioned shift in mentality and the potential for conflict accumulated as a social consequence of unification, the unscrupulous exploitation of the asylum topic has even intensified the hatred of foreigners and increased anti-Semitism, which are growing anyway. There are no simple solutions to the immigration problem. But no matter what position one takes regarding the change in the right of asylum that the Bundestag passed, two things are necessary. First, we need an immigration policy to make other legal options available, so that everyone who wants to immigrate does not have to apply for political asylum; secondly, we have to facilitate the naturalization of those foreigners who in the 1950s started coming in, chiefly from southern Europe, as 'guest workers,' and who live among us in the paradoxical role of Germans with a foreign passport – and who are now afraid of becoming victims of the kind of fire-bombings by the radical Right that occurred in Mölln and Solingen.

How can racism be fought in Germany and in Europe in general? Is it of the same kind as the racism of the 1930s?

To the second question I would answer both yes and no. Even though attacks and murders with a right-wing-terrorist background are occurring with disproportional frequency in eastern Germany, the catastrophic problems there, with a 40 percent unemployment rate in the now deindustrialized regions, at least afford an explanation. But in the western part of Germany, it is not the circumstances that have changed; the sluice gates opened, and the old prejudices that had been subjected to an informally effective censorship are now bubbling up again. However, the hatred of everything foreign and even just nonconforming has a genealogy that – by means of whatever unnoticed tradition – goes back to Nazi times and probably beyond. On the other hand, there is something wrong about the comparison with the 1930s. For since the early 1960s the political mentality in the Federal Republic has grown unmistakably more liberal. As a consequence of the student revolt, this change in attitude has become more extensive. The question is whether the old Federal Republic's political civilization will persist after reunification. A good indicator is the Federal Republic's orientation toward the West. Here I am thinking more of the intellectual than of the foreign-policy dimension of the ties to the West.

But the foreign-policy dimension is also important. What place should Germany assume within an international context?

We should push toward the political union of Europe, but not as we have up to now, administratively, without regard to the people. Because resistances are also on the rise in the Federal Republic, we need public dialogue about the further development of the European Community – which will probably pass by way of Maastricht, but which must seek a decisive democratization of the Brussels institutions and an effective political meshing of the national public spheres in Europe. Moreover, the Bundeswehr should participate in UN military operations, but we also ought try to get the UN to develop rapidly from a deliberative into an active organ. If the UN wants to be recognized as a neutral force that creates order, it must be able to conduct its operations with a force under its own command. Those are two examples of a program that could be prepared subcutaneously among us and that would contrast with an eastward-looking, sovereignty-conscious, militarized German foreign policy. What is in any case not good is the diffuse internal situation of the Federal Republic, in which the alternatives remain remarkably fuzzy. The spooky slogan 'Germany is becoming more German' currently expresses only a vague mood dampened by our internal problems.

The Germans' 'Sense of Being Special' Is Regenerating Hour by Hour: An Interview with the *Frankfurter Rundschau*

IF ONE LOOKS AROUND, *it might seem that theories nowadays reside on the other side of the moon. The pessimism of the older form of Critical Theory seems to be becoming truer than Gehlen's technological cease-fire and the beautiful world of the 'postmodern' – the abandonment of principles or the community of discourse.*

Those are striking formulations that don't hold. Gehlen's conceptions of a frozen condition of *post-histoire,* where all possibilities have been exhausted and nothing works any more, have more in common with Adorno's conceptions of a totally administered world than just a melancholic tone. And the postmodern arbitrariness, or its abandonment of all principles, among whose advocates you will not find me, is not lacking in descriptive content. For example, think of the mass of politicians who lose all sensitivity to the normative persistence of fundamental principles of justice when one mentions topics such as invasions of privacy, the right of asylum, UN military operations, and so on – in fact they lose sensitivity to the whole dimension of political power's self-control; in premature lockstep with the demands of a supposed reality, the political class goes beyond even the professionally necessary opportunism. All I mean by that is

'Die deutsche Sonderbewußtsein regeneriert sich von Stunde zu Stunde,' *Frankfurter Rundschau,* 12 June 1993. The interview was conducted by Wolfram Schütte and Thomas Assheuer.

that the labels attached to theories tend to say more about the history of misunderstandings than about the theories themselves. That also holds true for buzzwords such as 'discourse' or 'domination-free communication.' If you wish to concentrate, in the form of slogans, conclusions drawn from a theory, you at least have to relate them to the problems from which the theory starts out. I started from the black-on-black of the older Critical Theory, which had worked through experiences with fascism and Stalinism. Although our situation after 1945 was different, it was this disillusioned outlook on the driving forces of a self-destructive social dynamics that first led me to seek the sources of an individual's solidarity with others, which have not yet totally evaporated. It is the fate of others, even of foreigners, and not of the folks we know from home, whose fate must move us now, if we do not want to let it come to the point where we all have to share it.

Still, isn't Critical Theory bobbing like a nutshell on the ocean of unreason? Is the project of modernity still a project or only a defensive action – an effort to save the present from the future?

Alexander Kluge rightly speaks of the future's attack on the present. But wasn't modern consciousness always a crisis consciousness? That is, wasn't it always characterized by the fact that the present was put under pressure by the anticipation of too much future in the present? This is simply discouraging; I prefer encouraging alarmism in small matters. The 'interventionist' thinking that Adorno favored in spite of everything is repaid by small insights. A theory, in diagnosing its time, at most gets a grasp on contrary tendencies within a horizon laden with fears and hopes.

The devil keeps finding a new keyhole every day. What major influences did the 'Theory of Communicative Action' underestimate? Didn't it also underestimate the problems of distribution? Capitalism as an eternal subsystem whose accommodation civil society can count on?

The concept of 'communicative action' turns our attention to the binding energies of language, to the familiar background consensus, the reciprocal extension of trust and the more or less naive readiness for understanding on which we count in our everyday praxis. Pragmatism taught us to take common sense and the life-world seriously. But that does not mean praising this as the best of all possible worlds! The only reason the life-world became interesting to me from the standpoint of a theory of society is because its vulnerable infrastructure provides a yardstick for social crises. To put it differently: the life-world is the sounding board for crisis experiences. The fact that capitalism is just as insensitive to harming the moral equilibrium of society as technology is to the way it disturbs the ecological balance of nature is by now almost a cliché. Hence there is a practical need for the economic system to be reined in by the welfare state and ecologically restructured. That is easier said than done, because society is indebted for both its productivity and its permanent crisis to the uncoupling of self-directed systems from the life-world – the autonomizing of the rationalities of partial systems with regard to the imperatives of life-forms integrated by way of values, norms, and achievements of understanding is an ambiguous phenomenon.

Your last book, Between Facts and Norms, *is a philosophy of law. Earlier, you tended to focus on moral theory. Should we connect your interest in law with the insight that highly dif-*

71

ferentiated societies cannot be integrated normatively by way of the political public sphere? Did you underestimate the legal elements that guarantee freedom, and overestimate the self-determination of individuals?

Well, if morality becomes in a certain sense autonomous and, as happens in societies like ours, can no longer seek recourse in the substantial ethics of traditional duties – that is, if it lacks the support of religion or custom – then the individual's weak shoulders have to carry quite a load. Praxis doesn't gain much from the simple insight into what constitutes everyone's common interest. Then we realize that we have no good reason to act differently – but do we anyway? That is why positive law can also be understood as a functionally necessary supplement to an exacting morality that has been transformed into an individual conscience. The legal order of democratic constitutional states embodies a moral content, and for the realization of that content it is not dependent solely on the goodwill of those whom it addresses. However, the democratic procedure of legislating laws – which is what initially makes those addressed by the law into its authors – depends on an active, participatory citizenship and on motives that are not legally coercible. To that extent, the institutions of the constitutionally established state feed on the communicative interconnections of the political public spheres and on liberal traditions the legal system is unable to produce by itself.

Isn't the complexity of such a highly differentiated society the rock on which such a normative integration must go aground?

That is one of those questions that cannot be answered in the abstract, and that mislead the careless theoretician into making an a priori reply: the only way we can find that out is by means of a clever praxis that refuses to let itself be discouraged by false a prioris.

The objection made by systems theory is that the subsystems function only if their operation is not disturbed. That holds true for the law, too. How do you go about implementing moral principles?

Morality isn't implemented at all, we all learn it on our own if we grow up under halfway healthy conditions. The moral point of view is already contained in the structures of simple communicative actions in which we recognize each other as persons who are accountable and simultaneously vulnerable, and who need protection. Legality can be imagined as a transmission belt that conveys these structures of mutual recognition, which are familiar from concrete personal relationships, to abstract relationships between strangers. Studying judgments regarding fundamental principles, an important American legal theoretician, Ronald Dworkin, showed that law cannot do without morality: in difficult cases, judges need to untie the bundle of pragmatic, ethical, and moral grounds on which the political legislator has grounded the relevant norms – or could have grounded them. Positive law certainly speaks its own language, but it is not a morally neutral institution.

But it became clear from the example of the controversy about the use of German troops for reconnaissance flights over the former Yugoslavia that the executive prefers to connect up with court rulings.

I am not the only one who criticizes the German government as well as the decision of the German Constitutional

Court in this case. The court should not have agreed to hear the complaint brought before it and should have returned the political decision to the legislature; at least it should have done so if it considered itself – in accord with a procedural understanding of our legal order – a protector of a democratic legislative process and not as a keeper of a suprapositive order of substantial values. The high court ought to ensure that the democratic procedures for an inclusive shaping of opinion and will are obeyed, and ought not to take over the political legislator's role.

Isn't the perspective rather that of a harsh juridifying of politics? If you add to that the idea of a patriotic elite, then you have a constitutional state that is both operating on the base of a formally understood democracy and also programming itself.

In *Between Facts and Norms,* opposing this authoritarian conception of the constitutional state, which developed during the constitutional monarchy and is traditional in Germany, I tried to emphasize as strongly as I could the following thesis: there is no constitutional state without a radical democracy. This complement is not only normatively desirable but also conceptually necessary, for otherwise the autonomy of the legally constituted person is cut in half. If one takes seriously the idea of a community of free and equal legal persons, one cannot be content with a paternalistic legal order that provides everyone with the same private freedoms of action. Citizens can be certain of the equal distribution of subjective rights only when they have reached agreement as colegislators on the criteria and objectives according to which the same matters are treated in the same way and different matters are treated differently. For this reason alone, the democratic procedure that promises reasonable agreement possesses legitimating force. Thus the public autonomy of citizens, who create their own laws through democratic procedures forming opinion and will, is co-original with the private autonomy of the legal subjects bound by these laws. Procedurally understood, such a democracy cannot be mistaken for a merely formal one. At least I understand the procedure of deliberative politics as linking the use of administrative power back to the public use of communicative freedoms and preventing public administration from programming itself.

How can a society make itself collectively understood if the media for this self-determination are dominated by private capital? The serious print media are losing influence and the public's attention. The domination-free communication of the talk shows probably cannot be the model.

The introduction of private television has certainly lowered the general level of television programs. But looking at the content is a little too concretistic. The more complex the network and the greater the needed investments are, the more strongly a new type of power develops – the power of journalists and those on whom journalists are, or make themselves, dependent. The public's attention span and willingness to receive represent a limited resource for which more and more broadcast stations compete. That is why those who collect, select, edit, and present information – whether they want to or not – exercise control over the topics, commentaries, and authors that are made accessible to the mass-media-controlled public sphere. This power of the mass media has a political dimension and requires constitutional regulation. The German High Court has made a series of sensible decisions regarding media law. But clearly that does not suffice for democratically acceptable institutionalization.

What would the institutionalization of the Fourth Estate look like if we are not content with merely saying it ought to be institutionalized?

Basic principles for a media charter are continually being formulated. But the putting into operation of the lofty principles requires institutional imagination. I have not been concerned with that. If you think about the fact that on the input side of the media a very few major information producers determine the image of politics constructed by television, you might for example make use of an idea presented in another context, that of the neocorporatism debate. I mean the voucher system: the voters distribute, among a list of qualified applicants, a public fund to pay for citizen initiatives or opinion-formation associations that would otherwise have only marginal influence.

Then how can a 'bequeathed' public sphere be regenerated? Certainly not just by good persuasion. Political culture is not organizable. How do you propose to organize it?

Not at all. There exist more or less fortunate patterns of traditions, civilized forms of intercourse, socialization patterns, school systems, and so on. You can no more conjure a liberal political culture out of your hat than you can employ a network of voluntary associations to create an activist society of citizens. The idea that history could be fabricated was an illusion of the philosophy of history. Administrative power is not the right medium for the creation or even for the production of emancipated life-forms. The communicative structures of a life-world are constantly changing through the medium of communication. A functioning public sphere requires an intact private sphere as its flip side. An instructive model of this is a bourgeois public sphere recruited from private persons. On the other hand, there are nations where just such accommodating elements have been formed.

The objection might be: The life-world is already tied to the political system by means of the vote – and already produces political power.

Of course, the institutions of the constitutional state, together with our better political traditions, contain a portion of existing reason. But it depends on how we view democracy. For the fortunate heirs, who are defending the status quo, political voting is an institution that adds up the subjective preferences of all individuals in order to decide among competing elites. That is not entirely false, but if you understand democracy as an institution of deliberative politics, political elections are first of all an outcome of the public use of communicative freedoms. From this point of view, public opinion is shaped by informal discourse, whose influence condenses through the institution of general elections into political power. The political freedom to shape opinion and will is thus supposed to be exercised within deliberating and decision-taking bodies, according to democratic procedures that ground the presupposition of reasonable results. Such a conception is more exacting than the well-worn elite conception of competitive democracy; but it is in accord with a kind of politics that receives its innovative impulses almost exclusively from culturally mobilized public spheres.

Shouldn't one be scared silly by the new democratization movements, which, for example, bureaucratically petrify the educational reform of the integrated school?

Democratization movements have nothing totalitarian about them if they have to pass through the channels and procedures of a more or less discursive process of shaping the will in order to generate communicative power. But only someone who possesses administrative power can 'act.' Of course, reform impulses frequently peter out in the thicket of bureaucratic measures, because the implementation of new programs is not possible without continuous democratic participation on the part of those affected.

Doesn't one kind of fundamentalism elicit another? Some people are calling you an 'enlightenment-fundamentalist.' Isn't the universalism you represent blind to everything particular? Now the particular is taking its revenge by positing itself as absolute – ethnicity, skin color, nationalism; one could even understand the radicalism of the Right as something along that line.

There are different kinds of universalism. Thus we talk about universal or world religions, which make an exclusive truth claim for a certain doctrine and for an exemplary way of life. In opposition to them, modern sciences base themselves exclusively on methods and procedures designed to guarantee the validity of their results. Kantian moral concepts are formal in a similar manner as they underlie, for example, John Rawls's theory of justice or the ethics of discourse. Here all that matters is a procedure designed to guarantee the impartiality of judgment. This procedural rigor has nothing overpowering about it. It merely spells out the idea of equal rights and reciprocal recognition that also lies at the heart of any critique of the rape of the particular by the general. Because moral universalism demands equal respect for each and every person, it facilitates individualism – that is, the acknowledgment of the individual and the particular.

78

The critics' category error is connected with their choice of the wrong model; namely, the normalizing, leveling interventions of a bureaucracy insensitive to uniqueness and to individual rights in individual cases. But this is more closely related to certain qualities of the means of administrative power than to the normative idea of equal treatment.

Communitarians like Charles Taylor and Michael Walzer think that in some cases one needs to limit individual rights in favor of collective rights to prevent the suppression of cultural or national minorities – that is, collective identity as opposed to individualistic universalism.

I regard that as hasty conclusion. Our legal system is certainly designed for the private and public autonomy of individuals conceived as bearers of subjective rights. But these legal persons should not be imagined as individual atoms; they were individualized only on the way to socialization. If you take this intersubjective nature of the legal person into account, then there must also exist rights to cultural membership. Each person must be respected both as an individual and in the context of the cultural life-world in which he or she has developed his or her individuality – and that is perhaps the only place it can be maintained. These cultural membership rights, even though they are attributed to individuals, can result in extensive funding, public achievements, guarantees, and so forth.

After 1968, emancipation entered into a peculiar and involuntary alliance with the culture of 'experience' and with individualization. In the completed modern world the consumer is the last hero. Has the generation of 1968 failed to grasp the dialectic of its enlightenment?

I belong more to the generation of 1958, and cannot speak for the generation of 1968. I also have a somewhat more complex notion of what constitutes modernity, which we could not choose as a life-form, but to which there exist no recognizable alternatives today. This also has to do with achievements that modernity's self-destructive characteristics ought not to make us forget. A significant part of the old Federal Republic's political civilization was also connected with the modernization impulse, which the youth revolt energetically promoted even if it did not trigger it. When I read the tearful or cynical self-presentations of some of the people active in that period, I don't understand why they let Frau Seebacher-Brandt describe them as 'the generation that has been voted out.' The American SDS produced a very different bunch. What I find particularly annoying is the forced pragmatism of those who are again proclaiming the end of all ideologies only because they once believed their own revolutionary slogans. I'm not for ideologies either, but rather for the political clarification of alternatives.

People have asked often enough: What is the Left? In reply, we ask: What is the Right?

Today the neoconservative camp is differentiated into Liberals and Prussian-German-Nationalists. If we look at the intellectual scene, since November 1989 we have been discovering that there was always a moderately right-wing opposition to the Adenauer republic's Rhine-Union *[Rheinbund]*, although this opposition never quite got out from under the shadow of general anti-Communism and the resulting alliance to the West. It was no accident that we were reminded of this type of right-winger on the occasion of the hundredth anniversary of Friedrich Sieburg's birth. This side has always seen Germany's alliance with the West as mere political opportunism, never as reflecting the republic's intellectual affiliation with the West. These circles have always carefully cultivated the neoconservative legacy of Carl Schmitt, Ernst Jünger, Heidegger, Freyer, Gehlen, et al. However, they were sufficiently careful not to commit themselves as unconditionally to the postwar resentment of these now-out-of-step right-wing intellectuals as did Schmitt students like Armin Mohler and Bernd Willms, who remained permanently on the outside. But in 1989, these conservatives could abandon their restraint; and ever since they have been celebrating the farewell to the old Federal Republic and the return to the German continuities of a 'pre-eminent power in central Europe' no less unabashedly than their forward-dashing grandsons. The German 'sense of being special' is regenerating itself hour by hour. All the intellectual junk we had tossed overboard is being retrieved, and with an avant-gardish twist to boot – in order to have new answers ready for the New Germany.

The influence of right-wing radical think tanks on even the choice of reviewers for the Frankfurter Allgemeine Zeitung *speaks volumes. Is that merely a symptom in an economic crisis where integration through consumption is growing weaker?*

I am convinced that a polarization on the basis of clearly defined and well-grounded alternatives would still result in distinct support for the continuation of the better traditions of the old Federal Republic. But neither the intellectual Left nor even the left-wing parties are willing or able to instigate or fight out the long overdue self-understanding debate concerning the role of the expanded Federal Republic. Instead, the outposts of political culture are being unobtrusively moved back, and each new amendment of the constitution dries up more of its normative substance. The basic question as to whether we would prefer to forget the rupture of 1945 in favor of that of 1989 is not stated openly, but it is being surreptitiously answered in the affirmative – and with greater plausibility, as an opposition incapable of criticism allows a government incapable of action to muddle through mindlessly in all fundamental matters – such as the Maastricht Treaty, immigration, participation in UN military actions, or the solidarity pact. What needs to be discussed instead are the furtive fantasies about the new-old European superpower Germany that historians like Schöllgen and Weissman have long since been divulging.

The Adenauer Restoration's Debts:
An Interview with
the *Kölner Stadtanzeiger*

HERR HABERMAS, *a formulation that recurs like a leitmotif in your work is the claim that philosophers do not (now) 'have privileged access to truth.' What do they have access to, then?*

I have reservations about a certain elitist gesture of the German mandarins. Platonic scorn for 'the masses' was especially favored by German philosophers after Kant. Arnold Gehlen ironically spoke of the 'key attitude.' How many Heidegger fans are still laboring under the delusion that they hold the key to the 'exit from modernism'? But today, a philosophy that has for good reason become more sober operates between two opposite poles. As one scholarly discipline among others, philosophy deals with the rational foundations of action, speaking, and cognition, and in the process reconstructs an entirely ordinary, intuitive, utilitarian knowledge we are not even explicitly aware of using. Because of its affinity with 'common sense,' on the other hand, it maintains an intimate relationship to the entirety of our familiar life-world. This makes philosophers into specialists in the general; and ever since Socrates, philosophers have been going into the marketplace as well. Whereas other intellectuals seek to define the zeitgeist or to 'create' it, philosophers should seek rather to decipher a sybilline zeitgeist, as Hegel put it, 'to grasp their time in thought.' But

'Die Hypotheken der Adenauerschen Restauration,' *Kölner Stadtanzeiger*, 18 June 1994. The interview was conducted by Markus Schwering.

without sound knowledge there can be no sound diagnosis of our time. Kant – the only philosopher in the German tradition who is truly devoid of ambiguities – believed philosophers' vocation was to be 'public teachers of what is right'; he did not call them 'teachers of wisdom.' In their role as intellectuals, philosophers are best suited to translate the knowledge of experts, to introduce it into our everyday communications and to help make public discussions more precise, for example in discussions about 'working off' our national past, about abortion, about the right of asylum, and so on – why not?

One of your main works, The Theory of Communicative Action *(Theorie des kommunikativen Handelns, 1981), offers a very impressive demonstration of philosophy's 'new modesty.' A central aspect of this book is the abandonment of a materialist concept of reason in favor of a procedural one: reason proceeds through intersubjectively recognized rules of understanding between participants in a discourse. Some questions, however, remain. Here is a very pressing one: How is communicative action possible between subjects who are not 'backed up' by a common life-world? What can your theory do to help solve problems of intercultural understanding?*

Discourse theory in particular is capable of making a useful contribution in distinguishing between what philosophers call 'the good' and 'the just.' Our societies are also pluralistic in the sense that they promote and even mobilize the multiplicity of individual life-plans and the unfolding of different religious worldviews and subcultural life-orientations. These different conceptions of the *good* life, however, must be able to coexist with equal rights. That is why we need norms for a *just* way of living together that guarantee the

84

integrity of each and every person within the context of their own life-forms. One can say much the same about the Western world's difficulties in communicating with the other great cultures that grew out of independent traditions, and which can take pride in a world religion and civilization of their own. Philosophical hermeneutics makes it clear why intercultural understanding can be achieved only under conditions of complete symmetry. It is implicit in the concept of 'mutual understanding' [Verständigung] that each side must be open to learning from the other. Europeans can also learn from Africans – though it is difficult to fulfill such conditions for symmetry when the asymmetric conditions of exchange in the world economy reach into all aspects of life.

Doesn't the universalist claim you connect with human rights contain some form of intolerant Eurocentrism? You are obviously convinced that there is a fundamental consensus of values among peoples. But does that really exist? Just think of women's social position under Islam and in Western societies.

Nowadays the world market, the forms of communication, and all kinds of exchange and technology have brought all the states, cultures, and societies so close together that no one can get out of anyone's way any more. We have no choice: if we want to avoid regressing to atomistic tribal warfare we have to agree on certain rules for fair coexistence. An example is agreement on human rights, whose interpretation can then be debated, as it is currently being debated at the Human Rights Conference in Vienna. This normative idea of equal respect for everyone was developed in Europe, but it does not follow that it is merely a narrow-minded expression of European culture and Europe's will to assert itself. Human rights also depend on the reflexivity that enables us to step back from our own tradition and learn to understand others from their point of view. Europe produced more than a colonialism and an imperialism whose ugliness cannot be papered over. Occidental rationalism also produced the cognitive positions that allow us to take a self-critical attitude toward Eurocentrism. That of course does not mean that Europeans and Americans do not need members of Arabic, Asiatic, or African cultures to enlighten them concerning the blind spots of their peculiarly selective ways of reading the meaning of human rights. I consider this possible because different moral conceptions ultimately arose from common experiences of injured integrity and withheld recognition; that is, these concepts originate in very basic experiences in any halfway normal family. If the position of women in Islamic countries changed as it has in the Western world, because women want to emancipate themselves – what would be so terrible about that?

The Theory of Communicative Action *makes a decisive break with the Marxist tradition by relinquishing the fixation on the category of work as the quintessence of social action. How would you currently assess the Marxist components of your thinking?*

If we regard the nineteenth century from the vantage point of German idealism, we notice that Marx – along with Darwin, Nietzsche, and Freud – introduced the great sobering thrusts. Together with Kierkegaard and the American pragmatist Pierce, Marx is one of the decisive figures who set the course for philosophy after Hegel – that is, for all of us today. In particular, Marx offers us an angle of view from which the modern world ceases to appear two dimensional, purely linear, and manifests itself stereoscopically, as a split or fissured image: we cannot merely gaze into the mirror of modernism, we must also perceive its barbaric underside. In the course of his exposé of capitalism and bourgeois ideology, Marx never lost sight of this reference point; viz., the normative self-understanding of bourgeois societies expressed in the emancipatory ideas of self-confidence, self-determination, and self-realization. Marx was no 'postmodernist.' Of course, the theoretical foundations of Marx's critique of capitalism have been superseded. But an impartial analysis of the simultaneously liberating and uprooting, productive and destructive effects of our economic organization on the life-world is more essential today than ever before. The social achievements of the European labor movement over more than a hundred years are now supposed to be discarded in order to adjust the cost of indigenous jobs to the level of the low-wage countries. A governing party unabashedly promotes itself as the party of 'overachievers' and 'higher earners': We haven't had so much Social Darwinism since 1945.

You are generally regarded as the younger exponent of the highly respected Frankfurt School. Do you see yourself that way, or do you regard this entire construction of philosophical schools as foolish?

I was profoundly shaped by my time as Adorno's assistant and I stand within the tradition of the old Frankfurt School. But traditions remain alive only so long as they continue to be productively carried forward and even changed. The stimulating power of the 'Frankfurt School' (which was first called by that name when it no longer existed) was developed in several directions. No single person can be representative of all these developments.

Your intellectual biography is 'shot through' with controversies – from the 'Positivism Debate' to the 'Historians' Controversy.' What roles do these debates play for you?

I hope I have also learned something from my opponents.

Your latest work is a philosophy of law. Critics of Between Facts and Norms *noted – partly in surprise and partly in spite – what 'a pillar of the state' the book was. Is this assessment correct? Has Jürgen Habermas really become a 'conservative'?*

Other critics said that this was the 'most utopian' book I ever wrote. I am 'conservative' only with regard to the question that was raised after 1989, about the 'better' traditions of the old Federal Republic. The critical impulse in my theoretical works remains quite unimpaired. I wrote on the philosophy of law to make it clear to the conservatives, and also to our damned state-supporting legal establishment, that we cannot have or maintain a constitutional state without a radical democracy.

You have repeatedly emphasized that you regard Germany's unconditional opening to Western traditions as one of the central cultural achievements of its postwar history. This provoked Dahrendorf to call you 'Adenauer's true grandson.' Doesn't that make you sick to your stomach?

Looking back I see the true significance of Adenauer's *foreign* policy, which tied the Federal Republic to the West, more clearly than I did at the time. In the 1950s, I was outraged by the horrendous moral debts incurred by the domestic policies of Adenauer's restoration, by the cynical insensitivity to all the encumbrances he imposed, without a moment's thought, on our political culture. At that time there was not the kind of change of elites that has been so zealously carried out in the former GDR. The 'garden gnome' cultural climate Sieburg described did not produce the necessary cultural break with mentalities that went back to the Wilhelmine period, and continued through the Weimar Republic and the Nazi era right up until the beginning of the 1960s – a break that would have been so good for the spiritual health of the country. The cultural opening to the West had a hard enough time making its way through the stench of the Adenauer period. With regard to the intentional equation of cultural and political West-orientation, what counts today is to see the Federal Republic's 'Ties to the West' not as a clever foreign policy ploy, but rather as a way of breaking with the wrong continuities of our political culture. It remains to be seen whether that mode of thought has been truly revolutionized. Ernst Nolte is not the only one who is rediscovering Mussolini as an important avant-garde statesman. The *Frankfurter Allgemeine* feature pages are disseminating with approval the views of a former intellectual of the Italian Communist Party, according to whom 'the great culture of the twentieth century was mainly a right-wing culture: from Heidegger to Jünger, from Céline to Pound, from Eliot to Yeats, and why not, Gentile.' We shall see whether, after all these postmodern limbering-up exercises, the new right-wing myth of Germany as the land of the center caught in the 'pincers grip' of Americanism finds renewed resonance.

In contrast to the conventional national sense of identity, you designated 'patriotism of the constitution' as the only beneficial basis for a collective identity for the Germans. Now, this concept contains components that tend to go their separate ways. Essentially, the Federal Republic's constitution [or Basic Law, as it is also called] resembles those of its European neighbors and therefore cannot provide grounds for any sort of 'patriotism.' Can you resolve that contradiction?

The national sense of identity started to form in Germany at the beginning of the nineteenth century, during the war against Napoleon – that is, against an *external* enemy; in France, it emerged from a democratic revolution against *their own* king. Moreover, the national hopes of the educated German middle-class citizen – faced with a multitude of small states – had to attach themselves to an imaginary magnitude such as that of a *Kultur-Nation* rooted in traditions and language. It becomes easier to understand the bizarre circumstance of an ethnic concept of nationhood persisting in the Basic Law if we keep that historical background in mind. Carl Schmitt's ideas concerning the 'homogeneity' of the people of the state are now at last becoming fictitious. Closely examined, they were always fictions. That is why we finally need to learn to see ourselves as a nation composed not of people with a common racial and cultural heritage *[Volksgenossen],* but rather of citizens of a state. Given the plurality of their cultural ways of life, these citizens can rely only on their constitution to provide their common basis. As you said, the principles of the constitution have a universalist content that is not binding solely for Germans. Confronted by such an abstract order, only if we learn to see the democratic constitutional state as an important achievement within the context of our sometimes catastrophic national history can a durable loyalty anchored in motives and ideologies arise. It was not until 8 May 1985 – forty years after the end of the war – that a president of the Federal Republic comprehended the defeat of the Nazi regime within its historical context, as a liberation from dictatorship. So now we also regard D day as a turning point that has much the same meaning for Germans as for the Allies. Patriotic loyalty to the constitution requires a historical self-understanding of the nation that can support a liberal political culture.

The Left in the Federal Republic seems to be in an unenviable condition. It is defensive, it has had trouble dealing with the consequences of 1989, and it is riven by splinter groups. I refer to Martin Walser, Botho Strauß, Hans Magnus Enzensberger, and Wolf Biermann. How do you assess its situation and future?

The Left does not invariably invest the future with positive expectations: think of Adorno's negativism. But even when it is pessimistic and inclined to defend itself only against dramatic or dramatized dangers, it is acting with a view to a future. That is why it is particularly vulnerable to disappointments. The classical figure of the renegade, whose only way of working off his disappointment is to undergo a conversion, is only a mirror image of the orthodox people who dogmatically screen themselves off against dissonant experiences. The thickheaded incomprehension of a Heidegger or a Carl Schmitt belongs to the psychopathology of the Right, just as the compulsion to commit oneself is part of the psychology of the Left – though I do not want to attribute such compulsions to the people you just mentioned. The dejected reactions of former leftists to the disintegration of the Soviet Empire only shows the blindness of the delusions about state Socialism they had harbored. But this was by no means typical of the Left in the Federal Republic, which lived right next to the DDR and thus, in an entirely trivial manner, was prevented from having any illusions. What distinguishes the Left from the Right even now is an aggressive engagement with the ambivalences of discordant modernization processes that should drive us neither into resignation nor into adopting a reactionary attitude.

Recently you have interpreted the concept of 'socialism' in the sense of 'radical democracy.' Doesn't that go along with a terminological softening up that ultimately leads to the proverbial night in which all cats are gray?

Modern societies are held together by money, administrative power, and solidarity. Solidarity is perhaps too big a word for everyday communicative actions, for routines of mutual understanding, for tacit orientations toward values and norms, for more or less discursive debates in the public sphere. Socialism has always placed its hopes on the third of those sources of social integration. Along with Soviet imperialism went down a bureaucratic state Socialism that we call by that name because it set out from the faulty premise that by using state power, it could create by force living conditions characterized by solidarity. When I stress the radical meaning of our democratic constitution, when I draw attention to the basis of an association of free and equal legal persons conducting their common life in accord with freely self-determined norms, I am once again focusing on that third resource, which is also endangered in our society – on a solidarity contained in legal structures, and that must regenerate itself from halfway-intact life-world contexts. My theoretical works also have as their vanishing point the demand for conditions that are worthy of human beings, in which an acceptable balance between money, power, and solidarity can come into normal practice.

4. The Need for German Continuities

A Letter to Christa Wolf

DEAR CHRISTA WOLF,

I am grateful for your invitation to attend the meeting at the academy last Thursday. Jens Reich's thoughtful talk and the wide-ranging spectrum of contributions from a group of prominent people were revelatory of the moods and conflicts of those who contributed most actively to the change in the GDR. As a visitor from the West, naturally I felt a bit like a spectator gazing down from his box on a dramatic scene. What especially touched me was the persistent discussion about the 'zero hour.' It was remarkable how people's spirits caught fire at this expression, which the audience itself had put into the speaker's mouth and which did not quite correspond to the tenor of his talk.

I can well understand that sense of having tossed the old baggage overboard and standing at a new beginning. The intellectuals in East Germany are justified in feeling that they have been caught up in exceptional events and gone through an experience that is far from everyday. They are so powerfully drawn into the maelstrom of speeded-up life-histories that it makes us eager to see how they will digest this confrontation – especially the younger ones whose thresholds are still wide open. Our generation, too, dear

The 'Letter to Christa Wolf' of 26 November 1991 goes back to a discussion in the (then still existing) East Berlin Academy of the Arts. It appeared, together with Christa Wolf's reply, in Christa Wolf, *Auf dem Weg nach Tabou* (Cologne, 1994), 140–49.

Ms. Wolf, worked off the years before and after 1945 – they afforded sufficient material for a whole lifetime. On the other hand, the 'zero hour' discussions also contained something incredible. In deciding to adopt the West German currency and its civil legal order, the East German population did more than 'join' the Federal Republic in the legal constitutional sense. The mode of the unification could not be better symbolized than by the unequal pair of twins Schäuble/Krause: with what these two have hatched the course has been set in such a way that those who were eager to join can now only conform or submit; in any case, there is no room for political action. The image of a precipitous self-sacrifice that thus emerged is probably not entirely inaccurate.

But the fact that it will not be easy to make a new beginning makes it all the more urgent for those who are not in the mainstream in either the East or the West to establish mutual understanding and cooperation. My wish arises less from a desire for a coalition – you will soon get used to the fact that the right wing denounces left-wing intellectuals here as well as there. However, we must find a way of coming together in the face of the regressive tendencies that Friedrich Schorlemmer's clear and decisive vote called by their name. Despite the fact that for forty years the SED regime's worn-out propaganda slogans inveighed against right-wing radicalism as an external danger, it has hatched these dangers under its own wings. Something from a 1930s and 1940s mentality seems to have been preserved. In any event, after reunification a critical mass of resentment was produced, which also changed mentalities in the West. As in the 1930s, German resentment naturally also reflects shifts in the international climate – I refer to the 'national fronts,' whose strength in all

Western countries is increasing daily, as well as the ghosts rising from their nineteenth-century graves in eastern European countries. But in postfascist Germany the same development does not necessarily have the same meaning.

In the old Federal Republic, the novelty of the situation consists primarily in the fact that elements of the extreme Right that had previously remained separate are now combining in an explosive mix: National Democrats and Republicans are uniting for the first time with a violence-prone youth scene of skinheads and hooligans, and around both of them twines an intricately branched, right-radical publicity network that more and more conservatives are joining in a more and more uninhibited manner. In the past decade, the edges were already starting to fray: the liberal-conservatives appear to have lost their touchiness concerning right-wing radicalism and German jingoism. All in all, the spirit hereabouts has shifted again: the liberals are becoming nationalistically liberal, the neoconservatives militantly German. Something that was still highly controversial during the Historians' Controversy has long since been decided: one may now speak of the 'two dictatorships' without having to differentiate between them. One ends up being pleased when the regime that based its industrial mass murder on racial motives is at least mentioned in the same breath with Stalinism. The subtler intellects have long since gone on to busy themselves with distinctions meant to clarify for us the human and civilized features of National Socialism. 'Auschwitz in our souls' – the inflationary use of a once painfully avoided word is part and parcel of the clearing-out process.

If – despite the specific experiences and impulses to renewal East German intellectuals may have over us – current opportunities for a *new* beginning in the Federal Republic probably lead only in the opposite direction, we should not underestimate what we might have won had the mental constitution of the new republic not shifted so far back to the right. Here we depend on the former GDR's liberal and left intellectuals to prevent the net of a halfway civil political culture from being torn apart by the new burdens. I do not in any way refer to the notorious 'costs of unification': I have in mind problems that will come from outside and intensify internal discords. If we react incorrectly to these problems, the inner constitution of the Federal Republic that was so painfully achieved in the postwar decades could be damaged, with dire consequences.

One of these problems – the economic migration from the south (and now also from the east), which the First World created and which is in any case inevitable, today serves as a litmus test for our future reactions. Are we in the process of terminating the welfare-state compromise? Have we already gotten used to the idea of living with an underclass of from 20 to 30 percent? Is an affluent, chauvinistic majority going to toughen up externally and become repressive internally? Since at least the Reagan presidency, it has been possible to observe in the largest U.S. cities the way the 'ins' can survive only by means of a neurotic defense system that protects them from seeing the 'outs.' Are we, too, going to close our eyes to a structural minority of the disempowered, who have no opportunity to change their situation on their own, and whose only remaining means of protest are self-destructive? Are we going to accept a pattern of segmentation that makes a mockery of all the conceptions of social justice accepted as self-evident in the traditions of the Enlightenment and the workers' movement? Under progressively more stressful circumstances these questions will not find reasonable answers if right-wing populism spreads in the Federal Republic as well; the SPD and the CDU both simply adjust to it, while the FDP ignores its principles, and our 'green FDP' services the mentality only of left-wing renegades. The old bogey of anti-Communism that for so long continued to stabilize the collective identity during all sorts of crises has disintegrated – but the new bogeys are cast in the same old mould. The subtle constructions with which the grandsons of neoconservative grandfathers are fiddling in the feature pages of the newspapers are a first, distant echo of the rowdy slogans of the camp followers under the Reich's war banner.

This pessimistic assessment moved me to point out a consequence of the unification of the two states that, to my surprise, met with total incomprehension among intellectuals in the East. In the book of interviews I sent you when it was published, I said that the devaluation of our best and most fragile intellectual traditions was, for me, one of the most evil aspects of the legacy that the GDR brings into the expanded Federal Republic. The context in which I said this was unequivocal: 'The political rhetoric of the "workers' and farmers' state" was a misuse of progressive ideas in the service of political self-legitimation, cynically denying these ideals through its inhuman praxis and thus bringing them into disrepute. I'm afraid that this dialectic of devalution will end up being more ruinous for the spiritual hygiene of Germany than all the concentrated resentment of five or six generations of antienlightenment, anti-Semitic, false romantic, jingoistic obscurantists' (*The Past as Future* [*Vergangenheit als Zunkunft*] [Lincoln: University of Nebraska Press, 1994], 37). Richard Schröder and Friedrich Dieckmann reacted with absolute fury to this sentence. Why?

Is it possible that the misunderstanding that must exist

between us in this regard might have to do with an interpretation that was only barely touched on during the discussions this past Thursday, but which found precise expression in the 'Theses for a United Academy of Arts of Berlin-Brandenburg?' The text you gave me as we said good-bye states:

'Not only in the Eastern *but also in the Western* parts of a torn and divided Germany that was rigorously screened off within itself, there was a process of conforming to the mentality and culture of the respective world powers that dominated *both component states,* accommodations that left their mark and led to different identities for East and West Germans. The decades-long existence on a border that divides our own country and put its two parts in intense opposition to each other, acts to limit thinking *on both sides.* German existence in the form of two states has internally affected both parts of the population. It produced intellectual and emotional inhibitions in the East *and in the West,* inhibitions that, among other things, also led *both* sides to distance themselves in different ways from the power of the traditions of a once unified German culture.'

My italicizations indicate my doubts: I believe this peculiar convergence thesis creates the wrong kind of symmetry. Of course, some people in the West also propose this thesis; but it does not become any truer simply because prominent friends like Martin Walser and Dieter Henrich share your view. I am in no position to evaluate intellectual life-histories in the East; and if you regard your own literary production as 'inhibited,' I must leave that judgment to you. However, the judgment that our lives here in the West transpired under deforming limitations of the kind that you mention, I regard as false – and *dangerously* false, because it suggests the ugly conclusion that we ought to go back to those spiritual continuities against which we successfully defended ourselves – arduously enough and against the reigning climate – for the first time in recent German history. I would be astonished if we were to disagree about what traditions we should try to maintain – and which not. Please understand the following remarks as an attempt to confirm that consensus. I have always regarded the intellectual opening to Western traditions after 1945 as liberating. Some people may have experienced the division of the nation as more oppressive than others; but I can find no damage to anything West German intellectuals have produced during the postwar period; in any case, I do not find the characteristics you diagnose that might lead to the conclusion that some of us must have felt cut off from impulses that are worth keeping for our own existence.

Please do not misunderstand me. If I insist on distinctions in this regard, I do not under any circumstance wish to claim any special *merit* for one side while denying it to the other. We were born in the same year and we share the same 'childhood patterns.' Therefore we also share the basic attitude that, if I see this correctly, provided us with similar motives not only to make a clean break with the political legacy of the Nazi regime but also with the deeper-reaching intellectual roots of laudatory German mandarism and its murky German spirit. I can well imagine, and I have been dwelling on this since November 1989, that if I had not happened to have grown up in the Rhineland but instead found myself on the other side of the Elbe, I might even have identified myself with the antifascism of Communists who returned from exile, might have become a Communist Party member and set out on a career, and – since this is a hypothetical consideration – no one today could say when and where it might have ended. Ultimately, it was for reasons of that kind that I became a socialist even in Adenauer's Germany, which was not the usual thing to do; on reading the early Lukàcs, I discovered Western Marxism and made my own decision to become Adorno's assistant. Nor did I hesitate to write my dissertation under Wolfgang Abendroth. It is possible to give a most scrupulous account of all of that and yet find – without any suggestion of vanity – that we in West Germany lived under conditions that made possible, in intellectual matters as well, an orientation toward the West that was not in any way coerced or even inhibiting, but rather experienced as emancipatory.

This orientation toward the West did not involve a distortion of the German soul, but it did involve our getting used to an upright posture. The unconditional appropriation of the Enlightenment tradition in its entire breadth included, if I may use myself as example, American pragmatism from Peirce to Dewey, positive law from the seventeenth and eighteenth centuries up to and including Rawls and Dworkin, analytical philosophy, French positivism, French and American social scientists from Durkheim to Parsons. It also extended to what in the truly warped German tradition had been surpressed or marginalized until then: to Kant as an exponent and not as a so-called 'overcomer' of the Enlightenment, to Hegel as a radical interpreter and not as an opponent of the French Revolution, to Marx and Western Marxism, Freud and the Freudian Left, the Vienna Circle, Wittgenstein, and so on. The emigrants who returned from the West were more significant for us than our half-baked 'own people' who had managed to stay on through the Nazi period.

In this connection I recall the words my friend Albrecht Wellmer found some years ago during a conference on Critical Theory. They make it clear that the spontaneous turning to Western traditions in the 1950s was what first gave us access to the uncorrupted aspects of our own tradition. This would have been impossible had we relied on figures such as Heidegger, Jünger, or Carl Schmitt. One must first recognize the elements of the German tradition that are inimical to culture before one can learn to see the tradition's universalistic, enlightening, and subversive features as well. Wellmer explains the catalytic role of the members of the Frankfurt School who returned from American exile by the fact that they made it possible to envision 'a radical break with fascism without an equally radical break with the German cultural tradition; that is, without a radical break with our own cultural identity. I believe that the extraordinary, not only destructive but also liberating effect produced by Adorno and Horkheimer is explicable primarily through this peculiar constellation of factors. It was chiefly Adorno's truly rich postwar productivity that helped clear away the rubble beneath which German culture lay concealed and that allowed it to become visible again. He did this as a man of an urban civilization who was immune to the temptations of the archaic and yet maintained the romantic impulse in himself, and to whom the universalism of the modern was self-evident, though he did not overlook the traces of muting in the existing forms of humanism: a rare instance of a philosopher who adhered entirely *both* to modernism and to the German tradition.'

Lukàcs was certainly philosophizing with a hammer when he traced a 'path of irrationalism that led from Schelling to Hitler.' But even his crude way of proceeding could not conceal the element of truth in the very title of his book *The De-struction of Reason*. Wouldn't the effect of this act of cleansing self-reflection once again be squandered if the mixture of dull and deep thinking with which we had to contend for far too long were now to be regenerated? It is chiefly people like Syberberg and Bergfleth who are spreading among us the prejudice that we only conformed to the mentality of the victorious power, that even today we are 'intellectually and emotionally' inhibited. These people want to toss us back into the German swamp.

It is clear to me that nothing could be further from your mind and those of your friends. The transitional situation in which you find yourselves is accompanied by special vulnerabilities. This makes mutual understanding more complicated, and demands more than the usual tact in our intercourse with each other. I can see the exonerating moment contained in our relationship to a common fate. But premature acceptance of the symmetries urged on us derives from a false sense of consideration and only leads to new illusions. Therefore I ask that each side work off its own intellectual postwar history and guard against overgeneralizing its own experience. If we insist on tossing everything into the same German pot, the result might well be something none of us can possibly want: the history of the GDR could be swept under the rug of a historical account of a West German victory. I read articles in our newspapers that imply that the history of the GDR should be seen as part of a common German fate. But that isn't pertinent even to our generation – and still less to younger generations that today compose the majority of our population. We over here did not live under Stalinism and we are also not acquainted with the complex living conditions of a post-Stalinist society. It helps no one to force that kind of shoe onto our feet or to act as though our separate postwar histories were like a single *pair* of shoes. The only thing that helps in our mucked-up situation, as elsewhere, is differentiated observing and thinking.

For that reason I admire your effort to create within the framework of the academy of arts at least a substitute for the public sphere of your own that is lacking. The former GDR was deprived of the opportunity of initiating its own self-understanding discourse in the forums of its own public sphere, and not only since *Super-Illu* and Mühlfenzl. Now Western editorial offices are pulling the strings, and Western voices are louder than those from the East. At a minimum, the intellectuals – fully aware of the existing distances, and going beyond them – ought to arrive at an understanding. With the well-intentioned but premature appeal to presumed commonalities, we are only following a course set by others, and ratifying the mistakes of the Schäuble/Krause annexation-and-submission scenario.

Honestly hoping that we will soon find an opportunity, and that you will allow me, to continue our conversation face-to-face, I remain gratefully and with heartfelt good wishes, your *Jürgen Habermas*

Carl Schmitt in the Political Intellectual History of the Federal Republic

PUBLICATIONS on the life and work of the influential thinker Carl Schmitt have been piling up ever since his death in 1985. Aside from nationalistic portraits by his ideologically faithful students, there are the usual specialized scholarly monographs, as well as decent biographies that try to be objective. The terrain was prepared in the 1980s by the 'postmodernist' reception of his work, and since 1989 the situation has been propitious for Carl Schmitt: in the East, a need to catch up, and in the West, an open road for the entry drug leading to the dream of the strong state and the homogenous nation. The new Right had known this for quite some time: Carl Schmitt can lend a certain cachet to the topics of 'inner security,' 'overforeignization,' and 'excessive racial mixing.' The books by revisionist contemporary historians flowing off the Ullstein publishing house's assembly line mirror the virulence of the Carl Schmitt and Martin Heidegger interpretations of our era – as well as that very special mixture of Schmitt and Heidegger, from which Ernst Nolte's philosophy of history draws its inspiration.

Schmitt the political scientist and Heidegger the philosopher, both of whom had already acquired a deserved reputation during the Weimar period, can be related through the history of the effect their ideas have had. Although discred-

'Carl Schmitt in der politischen Geistesgeschichte der Bundesrepublik,' *Die Zeit,* 3 December 1993. (Originally a review of Dirk van Laak, *Gespräche in der Sicherheit des Schweigens* [Berlin: 1993].)

ited because of their spectacular support for the Nazis, and although in 1949 both had passed their most productive phase, Schmitt and Heidegger exerted an unmatched intellectual influence on the political and intellectual climate in the Federal Republic. Given the many differences in their ways of thought, their academic origin, interests, and fields, the parallels are nonetheless impressive.

They are spiritually united by an early exposure to the critique of modernity in a Roman Catholic milieu, a marriage that more or less estranged them from the church, their stubborn provincialism, and a certain insecurity in relation to everything urban, the generational life experience of World War I and the Versailles complex, as well as by the existentialist breakthrough from 'Goethe to Hölderlin' and especially the turn against humanism, a Latin-Catholic or Greek-new-pagan critique of Enlightenment traditions, whether under the sign of Donoso Cortez or Nietzsche, an intellectually elitist disdain for the party state, democracy, the public sphere, and discussion, scorn for everything egalitarian, a truly panicky fear of emancipation, and the search for an intact spiritual authority – and then, of course, by the Führer, who was to be their common fate.

Both men were among the 'great yea-sayers of 1933,' because both felt infinitely superior to the Nazis and wanted to 'lead the leader.' They recognized the delusionary quality of their bizarre plan, but *post festum* they refused publicly to admit their guilt or even their political mistake. 'Which was actually more indecent,' Carl Schmitt asks, 'supporting Hitler in 1933 or spitting on him in 1945?' This refusal, and his hatred of the 'preachers of atonement *[Bussprediger]* like Jaspers' stood at the origin of the incomparable effect Heidegger as well as Schmitt were to have on the Federal Republic.

There is no need to explain why prescriptive arguments, interpretive perspectives, and thoughts that find worldwide recognition are also understood as challenges in the Federal Republic; there are enough examples for a productive examination of these impulses. What needs to be explained, however, is the fact that these 'Reichswortführer' [spokesmen for the Reich] despite their incomprehension, and indeed their demonstrated inability to learn, could find the kind of intellectually fascinated following among younger Germans that indicates an identification with deeper-lying ideologies – and this in the country of a self-evident breach in civilization. In the case of Heidegger, whose teachings were transmitted by students who were not politically discredited, and who as a professor emeritus could go on teaching until 1967, the explanation may be trivial: he was known primarily only as the politically neutral author of *Time and Being,* and he adjusted to the model of a normality founded on repression and denial that was supported in German universities by a broad continuity in content and personalities that had unproblematically persisted through the Nazi period.

In Carl Schmitt's case things were different. He refused to undergo a de-Nazification process, so that he – an exception even among the heavily compromised jurists – was not granted permission to return to the university, even later on. The paths leading to the Third Reich collaborator who had been pushed out of office therefore led exclusively through the threshold of his home in Plettenberg, informal discussion sessions and circles of friends, and out-of-the-way colloquia and conferences that were held for 'the Master.' The barriers were higher, but the contacts were all the more inti-mate, the conversations all the more intense.

So there came into being an aura of something conspira-torial and initiatory, creating the impression that here a sub-versive subterranean current in the political intellectual his-tory of the Federal Republic had taken shape. In fact, many of the most intelligent and productive young people were converted to 'Schmittianism' during that time; however, ex-cept for a few outsiders like Armin Mohler, Hans-Joachim Arndt and Bernard Willms, they did not allow themselves to remain the permanent captives of the political prejudices of 'Benito Cereno.' They were able to make their career on this side of the CSU and the Siemens-Stiftung and made an anti-Communist Carl Schmitt part of the antitotalitarian back-ground consensus of the Federal Republic. However, all this still fails to explain why they identified themselves – despite not very inviting initial conditions – with such a figure at all.

This is the question Dirk van Laak – until recently in charge of the Carl Schmitt papers in the state archives in Düsseldorf – has taken up. In the process has emerged, from the perspective of a cultural historian primarily focused on the generational and group phenomena of 'interpretive elites,' part of the intellectual history of the early Federal Republic. The sociologically undemanding method of van Laak's 'research on small groups' is appropriate to the in-formal conversational groups in which postwar citizens and intellectuals in search of a direction came together. In addi-tion, some of these groups had the more practical objective of establishing contact and mutual aid among old, socially and intellectually dislocated Nazi Party members.

It is as such an 'ex-Nazi' group that van Laak describes the Academia Moralis founded in 1949. This officially registered club had formed around Carl Schmitt, and it also used industrial sources to support him financially until his application for a pension was granted in 1952. Aside from close friends such as Hans Barion and Gunther Krauss, former students like Werner Weber and Ernst Forsthof, and acquaintances from the 1930s and 1940s like Helmut Schelsky and Peter Scheibert, a historian specializing in Eastern Europe, came for lectures. One academy member writes to Schmitt in 1952 very much in the old spirit: he hopes Schmitt has noticed 'how wide is the circle of those who have considered it their duty to stand by you against black, red, and circumcised terror.' This letter excerpt, reproduced without commentary, evidently echoes the 'many kinds of terror' to which Schmitt felt exposed at that time (as he keeps repeating in *Ex Captivitate Salus* and in the *Glossarium*, those unspeakable jottings from the years 1947 to 1951).

Schmitt also resumed other contacts, such as those with Tat [The Deed] circle members Giselher Wirsing and Hans Zehrer, or with Margret Boveri, whom he knew from his Berlin days. In addition to offering sketches of several like-minded young conservatives – from Heidegger, Jünger, and Benn to Hans Freyer and Wilhelm Stapel – van Laak describes this circle's way of understanding the situation and itself after 1945: here a bit of ideology critique would not have harmed the analysis of the master mentality articulated in concepts such as comment, rank, character, and taste. The presentation of the reception of Schmitt in the academy in the 1950s also lacks analytic acumen because the author does not actually engage in reading texts and keeps his distance from the pertinent discussions in public and international law, in political science and sociology, history, and philosophy. The controversy about the concept of the political – reduced to Schmitt's foe-friend relationship – is superficial. Far more provocative for the self-understanding of the democratic constitutional state is Schmittian political theology, which rejects a secularized concept of politics and along with it democratic procedures as a basis for legitimating law, twists a concept of democracy that has been deprived of its deliberative heart into one involving merely the approval of the educated masses, opposes the myth of an aboriginal national unity to social pluralism, and denounces the universalism of human rights and human morality as a criminal fraud.

Van Laak describes in an interesting way Carl Schmitt's privately knit (or with the assistance of Joachim Ritter) network of relationships with the younger generation. Schmitt used personal contacts to acquire his most important students during the decade before 1968. In Heidelberg, Nicolaus Sombart and Hanno Kesting, whom Schmitt had known previously, led a closed circle of fascinated adherents who had been 'dissidents' in the Alfred Weber Seminar. In 1957, Forsthoff set up the Ebrach summer courses in which Hans Barion, Arnold Gehlen, Werner Conze, Franz Wieacker, Pascual Jordan, and other Schmitt friends also occasionally participated. These courses put 'the Master' in regular contact with a larger circle of interested students. That same year Schmitt came to Münster and inspired in an enduring way several of Ritter's most productive students – who of course absorbed his ideas at some remove and in their own way.

The ten biographical sketches at the end of the book show how Schmitt's ideas penetrated the intellectual development of two generations of students – who were, incidentally, exclusively male. The men who were born in the 1920s or later are of particular interest for the history of his influence on the Federal Republic.

Van Laak gives no reason for the selection of these successful portraits. It isn't quite clear why the author chose Hanno Kesting over Reinhart Koselleck, or Hermann Lübbe over Robert Spaeman, Roman Schnur over Ernst-Wolfgang Böckenförde, Rüdiger Altmann over Johannes Gross, and so on. Otherwise, the 'pillar of the state' aspect of this history of an impact would perhaps have become even more distinct. In any event, this list of illustrious names, which could be easily augmented with others taken from the index, speaks for itself: many conservatives, but not a whiff of the right-wing underground. It was certainly not in this fashion that Carl Schmitt destabilized the political culture of the Federal Republic. The divergent themes of neoconservative thinking these days are kept alive rather by intellectuals with an entirely different educational history; for instance, Hans Magnus Enzensberger, Karl Heinz Bohrer, or Botho Strauß.

This observation makes all the more urgent the question as to why Carl Schmitt was personally so attractive in the 1950s. The seductive power a brilliant intellect playing the self-stylized role of the outcast may have exercised on receptive, intellectually curious minds is hardly a sufficient explanation. These sensitive students encountered in Plettenberg a worldview distorted by projections and closed off by resentment. The *Glossarium* brims over with virulent anti-Semitism, with blind hatred of emigrants who are 'partially defective, from a moral point of view,' with the embarrassing self-pity of a man who sees himself as a 'hunted animal,' a Jonah spewn forth from the belly of the Leviathan. Schmitt was obviously pathologically incapable of judging the proportions of what happened and his own role in it; he denies everything and exculpates himself; he fulminates against the 'criminalizers in Nuremberg,' against 'the constructors of crimes against humanity and genocide'; he derisively says, 'Crimes against humanity are perpetrated by Germans. Crimes for humanity are perpetrated on Germans. That is the only difference. . . .'

Yet this Carl Schmitt appeared to the younger people, at least to some of them, as a figure who fulfilled two existential requirements: he seemed to make the causes of the defeat comprehensible, and he seemed to be a convincing representative of the continuity of a questionable German legacy. The young Sombart inquires in one letter, 'How was the defeat intellectually digested in Germany – is there a spiritual counterweight to the economic miracle?' And Kesting wishes Schmitt to be 'a secret prince in the invisible Reich of the German spirit' – he is supposed to be 'the advancing giant for all of us.' The most important presupposition underlying this expectation was the mutual feeling of having been 'defeated' in 1945.

The political consciousness of a generation may have been determined by the same problem, but not all its members reacted to it in the same way. Thus adjacent generations experienced and interpreted '1945' differently: for some, the date meant shameful defeat, and indeed the capitulation of the German people; for others, it meant liberation from a criminal regime – or at least a rupture they learned to see, in the light of the recently revealed mass crimes, as an opportunity to understand something. Those who as soldiers had risked their skins 'für Volk und Führer,' or at least for the Fatherland, probably found this insight more difficult to grasp than did others. Those who did not understand '1945' as a new beginning, as a challenge to make a break with the German sense of being special *[Sonderbewußtsein]*, were of course given the choice of adjusting unpretentiously to the new conditions. The defiance of the self-confident 'defeated,' embodied so grandly by Heidegger and Schmitt, apparently constituted an alternative, precisely for those who were more aware and went in search of enlightenment.

Anyone who follows this trail – which van Laak fails to pick up – a little further will see Carl Schmitt's attractiveness and his 'scapegoat's role' in a different light than he and his followers did.

Wolfgang Abendroth has already discerned the symptomatics of the rejection Schmitt encountered in 1949 when he made the futile attempt to be readmitted to the exclusive club of his peers, the 'Union of German Political Scientists.' They had to make an example of Schmitt if they did not want to risk stirring up the discredited past of colleagues and students who had long since been back 'in.' No settling of accounts and change of the elites took place in the early Federal Republic. The function of Carl Schmitt in the young republic's sociopsychological economy was that of a countermodel onto which the rehabilitated and the fellow travelers could projectively unload the repressed or silenced parts of their own life-histories – a functionally necessary supplement to the quiet reintegration of the old elite groups. On the other hand, Carl Schmitt was therefore superior to his privileged colleagues in one little-noted respect – and this may make the history of his enormous effect and his renewed relevance since 1989 more comprehensible: Schmitt, who never let himself be de-Nazified, did not have to remain silent; he was able to articulate German continuities with which others went on living, but about which they never spoke.

Under the pressure of the official opinion, dominant in the Federal Republic, the idea of 1945 as a decisive moment of turning away from the 'special German path' *[Sonderweg]* was finally grudgingly accepted by the Filbingers. The veil that was drawn over this skewed consciousness was of course lifted long ago in Weikersheim. But this divided consciousness was recently starkly illuminated once again by the editor of the *Deutsche Nationalzeitung,* when he revealed that Theodor Maunz – the former Bavarian minister of culture and world-renowned author of the definitive commentary on the German Basic Law, or constitution – had, under cover of a pseudonym, remained faithful to the ideology of his youth. Certainly Theodor Maunz and Carl Schmitt, the representative of the new state and the enemy of party-state pluralism, are two sides of the same coin: ironically, over the next generation they contributed, through a kind of division of labor, to a fundamental liberal-conservative understanding on the basis of which both have students sitting side by side as federal constitutional judges. But of these two men, only Carl Schmitt, only the one who defied the ruling political culture and dramatized himself as a defamed dissident, can make available the resources from which the reawakened need for German continuities can be satisfied.

In this I see a reason for that decade-long, bitter fight – which was not carried on solely in the *Frankfurter Allgemeine*'s feature pages – for the political and intellectual rehabilitation of the great neoconservative. It is precisely the specifically German offshoots of the lost First World War – which was also lost mentally – who appear as the true guardians of an unbroken national tradition. According to what they themselves profess, they had nothing to regret after 1945, for they felt that the movement they had supported in

1933 had let them down. They had seen National Socialism in the light of their own ideas, at least as a variation on what was 'their own.' Hitler, therefore, appears in Carl Schmitt's rearview mirror as a 'homeless down-and-out proletarian,' who broke into the 'temple of learning' and put 'pure ideas' into action with deadly seriousness. 'In return, feelings and formulas that up until then had been merely thought were surprised and glad to be taken seriously.' Schmitt's biographer Paul Noack therefore speaks of 'a kind of innocence of the German bourgeoisie, and especially of its intelligentsia, in the year 1933.'

Great world-historical events, as we have learned, always occur twice: the first time as tragedy, the second time as farce. And so it was probably the expression of a 'second innocence' of the German bourgeoisie and of its intelligentsia when the former president of the constitutional court – who had nevertheless been Theodor Maunz's assistant, co-worker, and colleague for many years – was confronted with his teacher's double life, and could only express thunderstruck astonishment at this deception.

Das Falsche im Eigenen:
On Benjamin and Adorno

SCHOLEM felt relieved when, in 1980, he could present his rediscovered 1933–1940 correspondence with Walter Benjamin: he also wanted to use it to defend himself against 'crude simplifications' regarding his attempts to 'persuade' Benjamin to move to Palestine. Adorno was to breathe a similar sigh of relief when he published his correspondence with Benjamin from the years 1928 to 1940 – letters that contain a convincing argument against the suspicions Hannah Arendt unleashed.

In these letters we see how concerned Teddie and Gretel Adorno are about Benjamin, who is becoming progressively more isolated and destitute in Paris; their energetic and unceasing attempts to improve the precarious situation of their discreet but querulous friend reveal a surprisingly pragmatic side of Adorno, who was not exactly blessed with worldly know-how. Nor can there be any doubt concerning the seriousness of Adorno's intention to persuade Benjamin to leave a threatened France while there was still time. This is further confirmed by an interview with the art historian Meyer Schapiro, recently published in the *Oxford Art Journal*. Shortly before the war, Schapiro, at the behest of Adorno and Horkheimer, had tried to convince Benjamin that he should move to New York. Benjamin was apparently reluc-

'Das Falsche im Eigenen,' *Die Zeit*, 23 September 1994. (Originally a review of *Theodor W. Adorno and Walter Benjamin, Briefwechsel 1928–1940* [Frankfurt am Main: 1994].)

tant to leave his European milieu: 'Well, he had already been invited by them. He didn't think he could be at home in America, granted the difference of his background and his interests.'

This is also in accord with a letter Gretel Adorno wrote to Benjamin at the same time (15 July 1939), in the tragic-ironic expectation of a reunion that would never take place: 'I am quite silly with happiness and constantly wonder in what order we should show you New York's attractions, so that you will also like it here among the barbarians.' In this, Benjamin could sense the slightly forced tone of suppressed homesickness; to do so he needed only to recall the ambivalent, romantic lines Gretel had sent him the year before, right after her arrival in New York: 'You don't need to go out of your way to find surrealistic things around here. . . . Early in the evening the skyscrapers are impressive, but later, when the offices are closed, they remind you of badly lighted European out-buildings. And just think, there are stars and a moon straight overhead and marvelous sunsets – just as during summer vacations in the great outdoors.'

Of course, from a backstairs perspective, one can seek out 'passages' in this correspondence in order to take delight in animosities that became more intense under the pressure of the struggle for survival and the marginalizing effects of emigration. In one instance, differences are mentioned that go deeper than mere 'irritation between correspondents.' To the latter, Adorno was hypersensitive throughout his life, and he is in these letters occasionally using harsh expressions he probably would have preferred not to have published. For instance, it is painful to see the way he dropped Kracauer, his old friend and mentor. But in general we find the familiar pattern. On one side, Benjamin, trying to keep his relationships – accompanied by mutual suspicion – with Scholem, Brecht, and Adorno separate, and to defend them against attacks from one side or another; on the other, Adorno, respecting the authority of a person like Scholem (whom he described ecstatically after first meeting him in New York) with uncharacteristic timidity, and attacking Brecht's 'shallow' materialism all the more insistently, making no attempt to conceal his sibling envy of Marcuse and Löwenthal, and putting greater and greater distance between himself and Bloch, especially after the latter expressed his view of Stalin's show trials. This pattern scarcely changed in the 1950s and 1960s.

At first, the correspondence with Benjamin seems to offer us nothing new in the way of theory, either; his philosophically most important fragments have long been familiar. What now lies before us for the first time as a chronologically ordered whole – save for a few lost pieces – must be justified in different ways. The reader witnesses a tension-filled process in which two persons, who had only this literary way of coming together more closely, grope toward each other. The partners in the exchange repeatedly assure each other that they want to meet in person and discuss things openly. Yet the chain of continuously postponed and aborted visits – Adorno made two brief side trips to Paris – not only reflects the adversity of the circumstances, but also betrays an unacknowledged preference for the detour through the written word. The formal requirements of the epistolary form seem to shelter a withdrawn Benjamin from the contingencies and importunities of direct contact and simultaneously afford Adorno – who is entirely engaged in the matter – greater freedom of critical expression.

Only once do we sense 'irritability between correspondents,' and that is in the letters that deal with Adorno's inaugural lecture as a privatdocent [unsalaried teacher] in Frankfurt. There Adorno deals with themes drawn from Benjamin's book on Baroque drama and – in an early, astonishingly far-sighted confrontation with Heidegger – productively sharpens them, without naming his source. This produced irritation on one side and, on the other, the idea of making amends by adding a motto or a dedication when the lecture was printed. In fact, the inaugural lecture was not published until after Adorno's death, without dedication or motto. Otherwise, the exchange, characterized by mutual caution and a certain elitist agreement, is driven by the amicable pressure that Adorno, from the start, put on Benjamin to complete the planned *Passagenarbeit*. A letter of 5 April 1934 closes with the words, 'Here I find myself once again repeating Ceterum Censeo: I refer to your "Arcades" ['Passagen,' a work that in fact was never finished, although it was eventually published], which must be written, completed, and done at any cost.'

Benjamin exerted a peculiar fascination on his friends through his 'metaphysical ingenuity,' which Scholem once called his 'most striking talent.' The spell that the 'Arcades' book, uncompleted as it was, cast on Adorno and no less on Scholem (right up to his death) is inexplicable without reference to the aura of an auspicious and enigmatic mind. The enthusiastic expectation Adorno connected with this project was projective in both senses of the word. Without even a grain of rhetorical exaggeration, he expects from Benjamin 'The piece of prima philosophia that has been set as our task,' and 'the decisive word that can be said philosophically today.' Benjamin does not contradict him: he sees this work as the actual if not the only reason 'not to lose one's courage in the existential fight.' However, Adorno's clamoring impatience also contains an element of *appropriation*.

Over the years, Adorno becomes for Benjamin – who opens himself only hesitantly to the younger man's almost impetuous admiration – a theoretical conscience, a kind of philosophical superego, because Adorno, at least so it seems, gradually acquires the power to define the direction the 'Arcades' book is to take. Against this background, the correspondence takes on a theoretical interest after all; the different variations of a common theme manifest themselves more distinctly than they did before.

What interests both men is the way the archaic is entwined with the modern; and the way one is depicted in the other is supposed to be determined – Bataille – by the dross and ruins, by the historically exfoliated 'thing-world of the nineteenth century.' In the archaic traits of the modern, which have coagulated into 'dialectical images,' Benjamin seeks to decipher two things: the destructive repetition of the old catastrophe, and an originary power directed against destructive modernism, which might turn the catastrophe around. Adorno finds suspect this second moment of the salvation and safeguarding of something aboriginal that first needs to be set free. For him, the archaic is produced historically, *without residue;* what history has silenced and disguised as 'prehistory' radiates a false magic.

Adorno denies himself any recourse to something aboriginal that could put modernism – to which he after all belongs – *entirely* in the wrong. Therefore he uses basic concepts such as 'reification,' 'exchange,' and 'use value' entirely differently from the way Benjamin uses them. Adorno is not a *Lebensphilosoph.* He resists the impulse to resolve the reified *entirely* into the spontaneous, to resolve commodity fetishism *only* into the devouring process of acquisition; his defense of the true aspect of the thing-form *[Dingform]* is not limited to the work of art – for only 'life that has been wronged in its thing-aspect *[dinghaft verkehrten]* has been promised an escape from the natural context.' In short, there is nothing aboriginal 'behind' modernism that is not indebted to modernism's own regressive tendencies.

A fundamental theme audible throughout the correspondence is Adorno's warning not to confuse 'dialectical' images with C. G. Jung's and Ludwig Klages's 'archaic' images: otherwise 'the disenchantment of the dialectical image would lead directly into unrefracted mythical thinking; thus Jung, here, and, over there, Klages, appear as a threat.' Adorno's repeated critique of Benjamin's 'anthropological materialism' continually takes the same line, especially with regard to Benjamin's neoconservative conceptual vocabulary. Adorno detects in his friend's texts even the slightest trace of giving an aura to *[Auratizierung]* aboriginal form, stance, gesture, corporality, and so forth. However, his critique only becomes massive in the case of the more distant Roger Callois, who, together with Bataille and Leiris, had founded a 'Collège de sociologie sacrée.' As though he had already sensed the direction Matthes & Seitz [a publishing firm] was to take, Adorno accuses Callois of 'an antihistorical belief in nature that is inimical to social analysis and in fact crypto-fascist and ultimately leads to a kind of people's community of biology and imagination.'

Benjamin nevertheless allows himself to be impressed by these reproofs, to the point of admitting that he has 'insufficiently overcome the archaic,' and (seemingly) agreeing to a plan to write an essay about C. G. Jung that would clarify the threshold separating 'archaic and dialectical images.'

Confronted by Adorno's repeated reminders, he finally takes refuge in Horkheimer's preference for the Baudelaire essay – in order to avoid having to settle accounts with Jung.

This tug-of-war around the conception of the 'Arcades' book manifests Adorno's autonomous philosophical intention. During the 1930s, he is acquiring a profile that does not fit the cliché according to which he assumed a mediating position between Horkheimer and Benjamin. Clearly Adorno is not only the philosophically trained person insisting that his quotation-collecting and collaging friend Benjamin delve into the material theoretically – while on the other hand he [Adorno] is removing the theological content from the speculative thought impulses he has received from Benjamin, in order to process them into a negativist philosophy of history with Horkheimer in Santa Monica, after Horkheimer, despairing of an interdisciplinary elaboration of a materialist theory of society, had sacrificed the *Zeitschrift*'s program in favor of a *Critique of Instrumental Reason*.

Although with Benjamin Adorno discovered 'the old as disguise and phantasmagoria within the new,' and although he even saw enlightenment turn into myth, at that time he was still far from wanting to salvage anything of a myth that had been thus deciphered. 'Understanding the commodity as a dialectical image means understanding it as a motif of its decline and sublation rather than as pure regression to something older.' Because Adorno understood the unity or 'all-in-one character' ('*In-eins*') of progress and decadence differently from Benjamin, he was immune to any superficial critique of progress. Nothing made Adorno more nervous than the 'mythical and archaiizing tendencies' of the 1930s, and – *Ach!* – not only the 1930s: 'Thus it seems to me that the category under which the archaic *comes up into* modernism is far less that of a golden age than that of a catastrophe.'

Surprisingly, even letters that were safe from censorship contain only the slightest mention of pressing political events. Moreover, both Benjamin and Adorno remained for a long time quite deluded in their assessment of the political situation. Not until 1938 does an apocalyptic mood begin to set in; and even then the events of the war appear to break upon Benjamin as an *unanticipated* catastrophe.

As apolitical as the two correspondents' views and judgments appear to us today – we who now 'know better' – the deeper levels of their theory communicate subterraneously with the catastrophe of the unforeseeable breach in civilization. This is still more clearly the case in the famous 'Theses on the Philosophy of History,' which Benjamin mentions just once, in a letter of 7 May 1940 (!). But what one cannot fail to notice is the political substance of Adorno's *differentiating* thinking, which he – with his unfailing sensitivity to dangers *nearest at hand* – exercises on Benjamin as well.

The disposition for this kind of critique of the false element within what is our own *[das Falsche im Eigenen]* is what explains the history of Adorno's later impact on the early years of the Federal Republic. Adorno made a generation of assistants, one or two generations of students, and an eager-to-learn public that read his essays and listened to his radio talks aware of the silencings and marginalized potentialities, the alienated and encapsulated elements within *our own* traditions. Albrecht Wellmer called Adorno that rare instance of a philosopher who belonged simultaneously to modernism *and* to the German tradition; and to this he attributes the liberating effect of Adorno's thinking, 'which was immune to the temptations of the archaic and yet retained the romantic impulse.'

Today the 'Western orientation' of the Federal Republic is again being challenged – the cultural orientation even more than the political. Adorno was able to draw the Western humanistic legacy out of the German tradition itself, because at the same time he brought its ambiguity to light. Using Kant and Marx, Heine and Freud, Karl Kraus, Schoenberg, and Kafka, he knew how go to against the grain of an anticultural, limitless, and corrupting cultivated humanism *[Bildungshumanismus]* as well as against staunch or exaggeratedly respectful antihumanism. For a long time, Germans did not forgive Heinrich Heine for knowing how to combine 'the party of flowers and nightingales' with that of revolution; they did not forgive him for stealing 'their' romantic legacy away from the fatally folkloristic *[volkstümlich]* and falsely historicizing, from transfiguring sentimentality – and returning it to its own, radical origins in the Enlightenment. The rancor Adorno encountered during his lifetime and that persists even today allows us presume a similar motive. For example, on the twenty-fifth anniversary of his death, the *Frankfurter Allgemeine* could come up with nothing better than a potpourri of hate-filled voices of malicious small minds. They cannot forgive Adorno's denunciation of false continuities, his ethnological eye for the barbaric in the most inward – that today, with our suspicious distance from our tradition, is precisely what offers us the possibility of identifying with our tradition.

Since the attempts – so cheerfully made by Syberberg, Bergfleth, Heiner Müller, Botho Strauß, et al. – to revive the neoconservative intellectual legacy, it becomes increasingly uncertain whether the Adorno tradition of critical self-assessment will be able to maintain itself in the bugle-call normality of the Berlin Republic.

5. Between Facts and Norms

A Conversation about Questions
of Political Theory

WHEN YOU ADDRESSED *the Spanish parliament in 1984 you talked about the 'exhaustion of utopian energies.' We live in a time, you said, marked by a 'new impossibility of taking an overall view' and by a negatively invested future* (Die Neue Un- übersichtlichkeit). *In our opinion this diagnosis has lost none of its relevance during the past ten years. The fall of so-called 'actually existing socialism' and the end of the Cold War have not led to a peaceful world. Instead we see ourselves confronted by civil wars, racism, new poverty, and almost completely unre- strained destruction of the environment. The hopes that the 'soft' revolution of 1989 instilled in quite a few people – Fukuyama even talked about 'the end of history' – were quickly revealed as delusions. With a view to these problems, in* Between Facts and Norms *you speak of a hope, born of despair, for the beginning of a universalist world order. Moreover, you hold fast to the socialist project. As the quintessential concept of the conditions necessary for an emancipated form of life – about which citi- zens must reach an understanding among themselves – social- ism can be achieved only in the form of radical democracy. In saying this, you turn decisively against any form of utopia as the outline and goal of a fully spelled-out, ideal form of life. What matters in the procedural concept of democracy you have*

'Ein Gespräch über Fragen der politischen Theorie,' *Res Publica* 3 (1994): 36–58 (in Swedish); *Krisis*, no. 57 (1994): 75–85 (in Dutch). The discussion took place in February 1993. The questions were asked by a Swedish col- league, Mikael Carleheden, and a Dutch colleague, René Gabriels.

131

developed is the formal characterization of necessary conditions for the unpredictable forms of a successful life. In the preface to Between Facts and Norms, *you write about the insight 'that under the sign of an entirely secularized politics a constitutional state is neither obtainable nor maintainable without radical democracy.' But is radical democracy even achievable? The question arises whether the realization of the necessary conditions of a democratic society – for example, equal opportunity for participation – is not too utopian in light of the previously mentioned problems and increasing social complexity. Would you agree with the thesis that the open-ended character of the 'modernist project' does in fact lack a utopian goal, yet cannot get along without utopian energies?*

Of course, the thorn of skepticism must have penetrated deeply enough into the normative flesh for us not to end up once again merely arguing for the adoption of lofty democratic principles. As you say yourself: a skeptical evaluation of current world conditions is the background for my reflections. That is why my way can be distinguished from purely normative conceptions such as John Rawls's theory of justice, admirable as it is in itself.

First of all, I am seeking a *reconstructive* analysis, in order to prove what we always already tacitly assume, if we participate in the democratic and constitutional practices that have fortunately taken hold in our countries. A consciousness that has become completely cynical is incompatible with such practices – unless the practices were altered beyond recognition. As soon as the normative substance goes up in smoke – for instance, as soon as people feel they no longer have a chance of getting justice from the courts, as soon as voters no longer believe their voice can in any way influence government policy – law has to be transformed into an instrument of behavior control; and democratic majority decision turns into an inconsequential spectacle of deception and self-deception. A capitulation of constitutional principles in the face of overwhelming societal complexity cannot be ruled out. Should this occur, our concepts of justice and democracy will change, and citizens' normative self-understanding, which still exists in our latitudes today, will undergo a radical transformation. Because such conceptual interconnections explain social facts, it is worthwhile to undertake a reconstruction of the interrelated implications of a legal system that can draw its legitimacy only from the idea of self-legislation.

Secondly, I try to show that this normative self-understanding of our established practices is not from the start illusory. I see these democratic constitutions as so many projects on which legislators, along with the legal and administrative system, work each and every day – and whose continuation is constantly being implicitly fought for in the public political sphere. However, we have to let go of interpretations that have become dear to us, including the idea that radical democracy is a form of self-administering socialism. Only a democracy that is understood in terms of communications theory is feasible under the conditions of complex societies. In this instance, the relationship of center and periphery must be reversed: in my model the forms of communication in a civil society, which grow out of an intact private sphere, along with the communicative stream of a vital public sphere embedded in a liberal political culture, are what chiefly bear the burden of normative expectations. That is why you are right – nothing will change without the intervening, effective, innovative energy of social movements, and without the utopian images and energies that motivate such movements. But that does not mean that theory itself, as in Ernst Bloch's work, must take the place of utopias.

You criticized the republican idea of a radical democracy because, among other things, it cannot account for the inalienably systemic character and peculiar dynamics of politics. According to your view, politics should be analyzed not only in terms of a theory of action, but also in terms of a theory of systems. Popular sovereignty in the sense of self-determination programmed through laws rests on opinion- and will-formation involving communicative action, as well as on a political system directed via the medium of power. This raises the question as to how citizens can influence the political system through processes of opinion- and will-formation without simultaneously impairing the system's inherent dynamics. You developed two models for answering this question. The 'siege model' you proposed in Volkssouveranität als Verfahren *(1988), corresponded to the bi-level concept of society in* Theory of Communicative Action. *This model implies that citizens besiege the 'political fortress' by means of political discourses that seek to influence processes of judgment and decision making without intending actually to take it over. In* Between Facts and Norms *your starting point is a 'sluice model,' in which the constituted political system consists of a center and a periphery. In order for citizens to influence the center, that is parliament, the courts, and the administration, the communication of influences has to pass from the periphery through the sluices of democratic and constitutional procedures. In the political circulatory system, law is the medium through which communicative power is transformed into administrative power. Now, in what respect does*

the precise status of this bi-level social model in Between Facts
and Norms *differ from that of the model proposed in* Theory
of Communicative Action? *Don't your two metaphors – 'siege'
and 'sluice' – imply different connections between systems and
life-world? According to the 'siege' model, democracy seems to
be little more than a way of limiting the imperatives of a capitalist economy and of a paternalistic social state. . . . Doesn't
the sluice model permit a much more far-reaching democratization of the economy and of political administration than does
the siege model?*

At the time, my purpose in proposing the image of a 'siege'
of the bureaucratic power of public administrations by citizens making use of communicative power was to oppose the
classic idea of revolution – the conquest and destruction of
state power. The unfettered communicative freedoms of citizens are supposed to become effective through – as Rawls
says with Kant – the 'public use of reason.' But the 'influence' of the opinions that compete in the political sphere,
and communicative power formed by means of democratic
procedures on the horizon of the public sphere, can become
effective only if they affect administrative power – so as to
program and control it – without intending to take it over.
On the other hand, the siege model is too defeatist, at least
if you understand the division of powers in such a way that
administrative and judicial authorities *employing* the law are
to have limited access to the grounds mobilized in their full
scope by legislative authorities in justifying their decisions.
Today, the matters that need regulation are often such that
the political legislator is in no position sufficiently to regulate them in advance. In such cases, it is up to administrative and judicial authorities to give them concrete form and

to continue their legal development, and these require discourses that have to do with grounding rather than with application. However, to be legitimate, this implicit subsidiary legislation [Nebengesetzgebung] also requires different forms of participation – a part of the democratic will-formation must make its way into the administration itself, and the judiciary that creates subsidiary laws must justify itself in the wider forum of a critique of law. In this respect, the sluice model counts on a more far-reaching democratization than the siege model does.

You distinguish between politics as a form of will- and opinion-formation, on one hand, and as administration on the other. These two forms of politics correspond to a conceptual division of political power into communicative and administrative power. One of the presuppositions of modern democracies seems to be that parliaments and the political parties are important institutions of will- and opinion-formation. But parliaments are now largely dominated by political parties that are primarily oriented toward the acquisition of power in order to govern. Various sociological studies have shown that the professionalization of politics, the growing gap between representatives and the represented – along with the commercialization of election campaigns – have led modern politicians to adopt a more strategic stance. For that reason, the room for deliberative politics keeps shrinking. To what extent can we still regard parliaments and political parties as institutions of opinion- and will-formation? And confronted by populism from 'above' and 'below' – to use Klaus von Beyme's language – how is it possible to control the political class in the party-state according to the principle of a radical democracy? Doesn't it seem necessary that the political system, precisely in order to maintain its in-

herent dynamics, be further democratized – that is, that more
room for communicative power be created?

My analysis was intended suggest that conclusion. Insofar as
political parties have been governmentalized *[verstaatlicht]*
in the interim – insofar as their democratic substance has
been internally exhausted – they are acting from the point
of view of the administrative system within which they have
established positions of power that they want to keep. The
function they should primarily exercise – namely, the articulation and mediation of the process of shaping political
opinion and will – they then fulfill only in the form of advertising campaigns. Thus they come into the public sphere
as invaders from outside rather than operating from its center. The various functions the political parties fulfill must
be more sharply differentiated. As Lefort rightfully says, in
a democracy the symbolic place of politics should remain
unoccupied: but it remains vacant only if democratic party
leaders are regarded as people's representatives and not as
officeholders or as potential administrative chiefs. This requires institutional imagination. The institutional measures
that help increase the political parties' 'participation' in the
formation of the political will, and could keep them from
acting as organs of the state, would have to be in place at all
levels – beginning with the organizational part of the constitution and going on to matters relating to plebiscites and
even party bylaws.

In your essay 'Technologie und Wissenschaft als Ideologie' you
write that since the end of the nineteenth century 'a growing
interdependence of research and technology . . . has made sci-
ence the primary productive power.' Nonetheless, scientific and
technological developments are largely excluded from demo-

cratic codetermination and control. Decisions reached within the realm of science and technology, and whose transfer can have unforeseeable and sometimes unwanted consequences for all human beings (for example, decisions regarding nuclear power and genetic technology) are only rarely subjected to democratic principles. In view of the tendency for political decisions to become more scientific and the great interest taken by business in technological know-how, the shaping of many areas of society is largely in the hands of experts. We might ask how that definitional power could be democratically controlled and tamed, so as to exclude the threat of an 'expertocracy.' It is worth noting that your early work focused explicitly on topics such as 'the relationship between democracy and technology,' 'scientified political and public opinion,' and 'the danger of an expertocracy' – topics that have no systematic role in your most recently developed model of the political circulation of power. Is there a reason for that? Where would you situate the definitional power of science and technology within your model of the circulation of power? How could and must the danger of an 'expertocracy' be limited?

The differentiation among expert cultures that I described in *Theory of Communicative Action* is accompanied by risks running in the opposite direction – on one hand, the threat of an introverted encapsulation that hinders the spread of cultural knowledge and allows everyday communicative practice to dry up; and on the other, control over decisions that ought to be arrived at democratically exercised by those who understand the issues – that is, the danger of an expertocracy that concerns you. To be sure, the definitional power of science and technology is in this regard a relevant subject. I did not discuss it in my most recent book because today, in contrast to the situation in the 1960s, technocracy theories no longer play a role in the social sciences, and the planning craze and a naive belief in science have evaporated. In the broader public sphere, critical attitudes toward science have almost become the fashion. This shift in the climate of public opinion has had some positive consequences, as the growing awareness regarding the dangers of atomic and genetic technology shows. The evaluation of technological consequences has been effectively thematized in various arenas. In the process, a praxis of counterexpertise has become accepted, which recognizes that 'science' is itself not a neutral authority and that the scientific enterprise is anything but monolithic – it splits into many competing conceptions that are also impregnated with values. These starting points for a politically related alternative science should be further developed and lent more weight in the public sphere and in parliamentary work. There are no questions so specialized that they cannot be translated when it is politically relevant to do so, and even adapted in such a way as to make it possible for the alternatives experts discuss to be rationally debated in a broader public forum as well. In a democracy, expertise can have no political privilege.

In your Theory of Communicative Action *you claim that unresolvable tensions separate capitalism and democracy. The self-understanding of modern societies expressed in democratic constitutional principles implies de jure the primacy of the lifeworld with regard to the subsystem represented by the economy and the state. This primacy, however, is undermined de facto by the neutralization of social inequalities, which are inscribed in capitalism in the form of paternalistic social services provided by the state. Citizens of the state frequently no longer see or rather perceive the possibilities of political participation in-herent in citizenship. If we understand correctly, the emphasis in* Between Facts and Norms *is on the axis 'life-world/state' rather than on the axis 'life-world/economy.' Compared with your earlier writings, in this book you devote little space to the problem of how the destructive forces of the capitalist econ-omy can be democratically contained. Yet there are indications that the end of actually existing socialism is capable of lending the critique of capitalism a new impetus – as is shown, for in-stance, by the work of Friedrich Kambartel and Claus Offe on market socialism and a guaranteed basic income. Is your re-spect for the inherent systematic dynamics of a market-driven economy compatible with your conception of a deliberative poli-tics and an ecological domestication of capitalism? In view of the tensions that exist between capitalism, ecology, and democ-racy, doesn't it become necessary to differentiate the concept of an inherent dynamics into a positive-exonerating one and a negative-destructive one? In what relationship do you think do capitalism, ecology, and democracy stand to each other? Con-fronted by a progressive destruction of the environment and a society in which the work to be distributed is becoming increas-ingly scarcer, wouldn't it be possible, on the basis of the system of basic rights you have developed, to justify a legally guar-anteed basic income and to enlist a basic right to equal living conditions as a justification for a basic income? Faced with 'the end of the society of work' (André Gorz) isn't a basic income needed so as to provide the degree of self-respect and autonomy necessary for a properly functioning democracy?*

The point of the analysis of social modernization developed in *Theory of Communicative Action* was precisely to clarify the distinction you mention. We have to acknowledge the differentiation benefits of a capitalist economy, without concealing or accepting as a natural fate the social, cultural, and ecological costs that arise from a certain organization of economic production. I am interested in the processes of exchange that flow in both directions between life-world and system – as well as in the colonizing incursions of the money medium into communicatively structured realms of life, and the possibilities of damming up the inherently destructive dynamic of the economic system for the sake of environmental imperatives. From this theoretical perspective, the bankruptcy of state Socialism – that is, of the attempt to replace the directive function of money by extensive administration – cannot come as a surprise; but that is not to say that the historical events of 1989 did not surprise me.

On the other hand, the social theories developed in the Marxist tradition were too narrowly based on crisis analyses, so that constructive models are lacking today. All of us are rather at a loss as we confront the destructive consequences of a worldwide capitalism whose productivity we do not want to give up. That explains the renewed relevance of purely normatively based models for a 'market socialism.' These models pick up the correct idea of retaining a market economy's effective steering effects and impulses to innovation without at the same time accepting the negative consequences of a systematically reproduced unequal distribution of 'bads' and 'goods.' The crux of all these models is of course the vanishing possibilities for action. The old nation-state's political capacity for action (and also that of the newer nation-combines, and of the permanently established international bodies) stands in no relationship to the self-steering mechanism of the global market network. The problems of a long overdue reorganization of world economic relationships therefore throw a new light on the desperate condition of international relations, and the role of the UN and other world organizations.

The idea of a guaranteed basic income discussed in the 1980s certainly has the interesting aspect that the material basis for citizens' self-respect and political autonomy would be made independent of the more or less contingent success of the private individual on the labor market. But these matters probably can be meaningfully judged only within the context of the complicated tasks of a reconstruction of the welfare state, which is in danger of being dismantled.

The critique made by dissidents and by the peacefully operating Citizens' Rights movement in eastern and central Europe lay at the foundation of the revolutionary events of 1989 and helped bring the concept of 'civil society' quickly into vogue among intellectuals in the West. This concept acquired a positive connotation because of its connection with the dissidents and the Citizens' Rights movement. You understand civil society as 'the nonstate and noneconomic interconnections and voluntary associations that anchor the communication structures of the public sphere in social components of the life-world. Civil society is composed of these more or less spontaneously created associations, organizations, and movements, which locate, absorb, condense, amplify, and carry on into the political public sphere the response societal problems find in the realms of private life.' You claim that the political public sphere can find its sole support in a civil society 'that has moved beyond class demarcations and thrown off the millennia-old shackles of social stratifications and exploitations.' Doesn't this invite an empirical critique that would point out that the public sphere is not only dominated by media power but its civil-societal basis is still marked by inequalities of class and gender that the new poverty has increased rather than lessened? With your ideas about a democratic public sphere, aren't you attributing to citizens a postconventional ego-identity that fails to correspond to the personality structure of most citizens? The response Shirinovsky finds in Russia, Le Pen in France, Schönhuber in Germany, and Allessandra Mussolini in Italy strengthens our impression that many citizens have a rather conventional ego-identity. The nationalistic regression shows that something other than democratic impulses also emanates from civil society. The concept of civil society has now also acquired a negative connotation because of right-wing pressure in the street. . . . How – on the basis of your discourse theory of justice and the democratic constitutional state – could one distinguish the undemocratic from the democratic impulses of civil society, and criticize them?

Well, if it is a matter of diagnosis, we can draw a sharp distinction, precisely from the point of view of a theory of communication, between populist mass mobilization in totalitarian states and democratic movements from the center of a civil society. Hannah Arendt already did so in her classic work *The Origin of Totalitarianism,* and she pointed to the important role played by the structures of the public sphere in this connection. Communicative power can be formed only in public spheres that produce intersubjective relationships on the basis of reciprocal recognition and make it possible to use communicative freedoms; that is, to take spontaneous positive or negative positions with regard to free-floating themes, grounds, and information. If these individualizing forms of an unimpaired intersubjectivity are destroyed, there arise masses of individuals who are 'isolated from each other' and who – once they are indoctrinated by leaders relying on plebiscites and set in motion – can then be provoked to participate in mass actions. Arendt's analysis was still designed for the forms of movement of collectives as we know them from the first half of our century – the classic mass demonstrations and mass strikes, the way the Nazi *Reichsparteitage* were conducted, military parades. In the posttotalitarian age of a Berlusconi, the image of the masses on the move has retreated behind the electronically interconnected network audience: even in 1989, the masses that revolted in front of party and government buildings acquired a different function when they were transformed into guests on live TV. So the images of the totalitarian state appear to have vanished, but the destructive potential of a *new* kind of massification has remained. In the public sphere of the media as well there are still structures that block a horizontal exchange of spontaneously taken positions – that is, the use of communicative freedoms – and simultaneously make the isolated and privatized viewers susceptible to an incapacitating collectivization of their conceptual worlds. Such *shaped* public spheres, which serve as forums for legitimation by plebiscite, differ from liberal public spheres in that the latter offer a vehicle for the authority of a *position-taking* public. Once a *public* starts moving, it does not march in unison, but rather offers the spectacle of anarchically unshackled communicative freedoms. In the simultaneously decentered and porous structures of the public sphere, the scattered critical potential is collected, activated, and bundled together. This certainly requires a civil social foundation. Social movements can then draw attention to certain subjects and dramatize certain contributions. In the process, the masses' dependency on populist leaders is turned around: the players in the arena are indebted for their influence to the approval they receive from a gallery that is trained in criticism.

Of course, a liberal public sphere requires a free form of association, domesticated media power, and the political culture of a population *accustomed* to freedom; it needs to be met halfway by a more or less rationalized life-world. To this correspond, on the side of personality structures, post-conventional ego-identities. You will now object that even we in the Western democracies must reckon with an entirely different state of consciousness. Dispositions continue to exist that make a considerable portion of an overstressed population susceptible to the Le Pens and Schönhubers, to nationalism and xenophobia. These facts are unchallengeable. But to what do they represent an objection? For it cannot be to the philosopher who – in the name of his normative theory and with the gesture of an impotent Ought – furthers a postconventional consciousness, thus sinning against a human nature that pessimistic anthropology has always led into battle against the intellectuals' dream dances. All we do is reconstruct the Ought that has immigrated into praxis itself, and we only need to observe that in positive law and the democratic constitutional state – that is, in the existing practices themselves – principles are embodied that depend on a postconventional grounding, and to that extent are tailored to the public consciousness of a liberal political culture. This normative self-understanding introduces into our relationships, which are not what they ought to be, a certain dynamics: we see the constitution as a project we can continue working on – or abandon in discouragement.

In Between Facts and Norms *you regard the ideal communication community as a model of 'pure' communicative social-*

ization. And in this connection you emphasize that one should not misunderstand the discursive character of the opinion- and will-formation essential for democracy by hypostatizising the ideal content of general argumentative presuppositions into a model of pure communicative socialization. However, the conception of an ideal communication community rests on idealizations. In our opinion, the idealizations can be interpreted in (at least) two ways. Thus the assumptions humans always make when they raise validity claims – including the assumption that their arguments convince others and are not for the time being contradicted – can be interpreted as idealizations. These idealizations do not of course exclude the possibility that there might be arguments that could lead people to revise their validity claims. According to a second interpretation, idealizations can refer to a final consensus and to the assumptions regarding communication in an ideal communicative society human beings anticipate when they raise validity claims. Albrecht Wellmer has pointed out that this second interpretation of idealizations does not make sense. If the ideal communication community were to be achieved at a future point in history it would mean the end of any form of human communication. In an ideal communication community, the conditions of the possibility of what is idealized are negated. In spite of this criticism, you have not given up the concept of the ideal communication community. The ideal communication community serves as a foil for detecting and articulating divergences from the model of pure communicative socializations. It can be used to make it possible to perceive the unavoidable elements of inertia that are inherent in the processes of opinion- and will-formation – for example, asymmetries in access to information as well as an unequal distribution of competencies and knowledge. If our view is correct, the model of pure communicative socialization is capable of two *different functions: first it can be of help if one wants to bring to light the unavoidable elements of inertia; and, secondly, it can be used as a normative yardstick for a critique of the existing power relationships in the political public sphere. Do we even need the concept of an ideal communication community, as you claim, in order to identify the unavoidable elements of inertia? Aren't the traditional sociological means sufficient for that? Or a philosophy like Foucault's? And in any event don't the various globalization processes see to it that the universal normative yardsticks crystallize out – yardsticks that are, of course, indispensable for a critique of society? In other words, doesn't the mounting cultural, ecological, and economic interdependence inevitably lead to the development of a common language 'that is necessary for the perception and the articulation of global social relevancies and norms' (Between Facts and Norms)? Couldn't we just as easily get along without the concept of an ideal communication community and simply retain the previously mentioned first interpretation of idealization?*

If you introduce the life-world and communicative action as complementary concepts and say that the life-world reproduces itself by means of communicative actions, then you lay values, norms, and especially the use of language oriented toward mutual understanding under a burden of integration they could bear only in a society that met the demands of the intentionalist mode of pure communicative socialization. I have already defended myself against this hermeneutic idealism in *Theory of Communicative Action*. Along with Bernhard Peters, I have now taken a different tack (in *Die Integration moderner Gesellschaften*, Frankfurt am Main, 1993) to indicate my reservations regarding such an idealist misunderstanding of social integration, which

147

some people incorrectly ascribe to me. Such reservations could also be expressed in terms of Luhmann's theory of systems or Foucault's theory of power. Instead, I make a methodological use of the notion of an 'ideal communication community' to make visible the inescapable elements of societal inertia. That cannot be the real point at issue.

Besides, like Wellmer, I criticize the conception of an ideal communication community as it was developed by Peirce and Apel, and even my own discourse on the 'ideal speech situation,' as examples of 'the fallacy of misplaced concreteness.' These images are concretist, because they suggest a final condition that might be achieved in time, which cannot be what they are intended to suggest. But I continue to insist on the idealizing content of the inescapable pragmatic presuppositions of a praxis from which only the better argument is supposed to emerge. After we have abandoned the correspondence concept of truth, the unconditional character of truth-claims can be explained only in relation to a 'justification under ideal conditions' (Putnam).

If we analyze the sense of 'truth' in terms of justification, we must avoid equating truth with rational acceptability; what was once accepted rationally as true can turn out to be false. We call an expression 'true' when we are convinced that it will withstand future objections – which does not exclude the possibility that we have made a mistake. But only if we consider propositions as *unconditionally* true, regardless of their fallibility, are we prepared to build bridges and board airplanes – that is, to assume the risks of acting on these propositions. However, this sense of unconditionality, which marks the difference between truth and rational acceptability, can be expressed in terms of justification only because we consider our justification praxis, that is, our argumentation, as in some respects a component of an ideal performance. Even today we must be able to form our convictions on the basis of the best available knowledge and arguments, without being coerced; that is, without being coerced except by the noncoercive coercion exercised by the better argument. In the section to which you allude in *Between Facts and Norms* I argue that 'the contra-factual presuppositions from which participants in an argument must set out open a perspective in which they can surmount the inescapable provinciality of their spatio-temporal context . . . and do justice to *transcending* validity claims. But with transcending validity claims they do not situate themselves in the transcendental Beyond of an ideal realm of intelligible beings.'

I also have to resort to such forms of argumentation in instances where validity claims can be resolved *discursively* if the legitimacy of law is to depend upon properties of the democratic process by which laws are made. Democratic procedure grounds a *presumption* of the reasonableness of results that have been achieved in conformity with procedures only when, if, and insofar as it guarantees – together with the legal institutionalization of corresponding forms of argumentation (and negotiations) – a discursive formation of opinion and will in the previously mentioned sense. Convincing normative yardsticks are formed only under such conditions. They are not simply produced naturally as a mere result of globalization processes.

The political public sphere is a place of equality only when it is formally considered; that is, the fact that every citizen has the same legal status in a particular state does not mean that there are also the same possibilities of influencing the formation of will and opinion. Political power is still unequally distributed according to class, gender, and ethnic membership. Examples include the emergence of an underclass in many democratic states, the underparticipation of women in politics, and the riots that occurred in Los Angeles after the acquittal of the policemen who mistreated Rodney King. To what extent is it possible, using your formal theory of political combat, to oppose not only a communitarian but also a Marxist critique of liberal formalism? What is your position on the question of quotas, for example for women or members of ethnic minorities, to increase their opportunities to participate in political power?

Struggles for recognition in the democratic constitutional state possess legitimate strength only to the extent that all groups find access to the political sphere, that they all speak up, that they are able to articulate their needs, and that no one is marginalized or excluded. From the viewpoint of representation and 'qualification for citizenship,' it is already important to secure the factual preconditions for equal opportunity to exercise formally equal rights. This is true not only for political participation, but also for social participation and for private rights to freedom, since no one can act in a politically autonomous fashion unless the conditions for private autonomy are guaranteed. In this connection I also support quotas: for example, I support a policy of 'preferred hiring' in all sectors of education and employment where that is the only way to secure the 'fair value' of equal rights for historically and structurally disadvantaged groups. These measures are intended to have 'a remedial effect' and are therefore only temporary in nature.

Considered from the point of view of the criteria for membership in modern democracies, people are members of a given society if they have citizens' rights. Consequently, the sovereignty of a people [Volkssouveränität] *relates to all human beings who have citizens' rights within a certain society. Citizens' rights are exclusive because they entail a differentiation between members and nonmembers, between citizens and foreigners. Since morally grounded human rights are not related to membership in a certain society, they are distinct from citizens' rights. Human rights are inclusive because – in contrast to citizens' rights, which, normally are bound to the territory of a nation-state – human rights have a transnational, universal character. Political philosophy still continues to debate the question – as in the case of the debate between liberals and communitarians – whether human rights and citizens' rights are in competition or mutually ground each other. As becomes apparent in the system of basic rights you have grounded in a theory of discourse, in your view there is an internal relationship between human rights and citizens' rights. This connection 'lies in the normative content of a way of exercising political autonomy guaranteed, not so much by the form of the general laws, as by the communicative form in which opinion and will are shaped discursively'* (Between Facts and Norms). *If we have understood you correctly, your derivation of the system of basic rights takes as its starting point the methodological fiction of a society without a state. Yet in harsh reality the positive legal status of human rights is precarious: many nation-states' positive legal systems are able to resist the moral pressure that emanates from these rights. So recourse to the sovereignty of a people legitimizes a situation that is unacceptable from the human rights perspective – the German 'asylum debate' being one example. Thus the question arises as to how one might be able to establish a bridge between the internal relationship between citizens' rights and human rights on the one hand, and, on the other hand, the area of conflict that actually exists between them. Do you see your system of rights as a critical foil used to denounce the precarious positive legal status of human rights? And can we establish, in the absence of a world society, a moral hierarchy of citizens' rights and human rights? Don't 'human dignity' and 'physical inviolability' – think of the example of the hot war that has succeeded the Cold War in the former Yugoslavia – have primacy in certain situations over a people's sovereignty? Isn't the status of human rights dependent on the realization of world-citizens' rights and the monopolization of force worldwide?*

You have asked several questions at once. First, I distinguish morally grounded *human* rights from legal human *rights* that have acquired positive validity through our constitutions; that is, they have been given a guarantee, within the pertinent legal order, that sanctions will be used to achieve them. It is because of their universal human rights content that these basic rights are pushing – as if on their own – toward the realization of a form of world citizenship in which human rights everywhere acquire the status and the validity of positive law. Such a situation cannot be achieved solely through international courts; for this we need a UN capable of reaching decisions and taking action, and that can, when it needs to intervene, employ military forces under its *own* command instead of delegating this function to the superpowers, which merely lend themselves UN legitimation for the conduct of their wars. The case is entirely different when valid basic rights are limited by parliamentary decision, and – as happened here in Germany in the case of the right to asylum – these rights are de facto hollowed out.

This is the case you mention in your second question as an example of an unfortunate competition between human and citizen rights – indeed, as a case in which the classic rights to freedom of life, liberty, and property are subordinated to the sovereignty of the legislative power. However, regarded normatively, the political legislative power is not permitted – in Germany or elsewhere – to limit or abolish absolute basic rights. The constitutional court can invalidate such decisions in the course of its review of norms. Whether the new asylum law is formulated so carefully as to withstand a constitutional court test is a question for experts, and I will not address it here.

Finally, you are interested in the relationship of a people's sovereignty to human rights in general. The example of the civil war in Bosnia, however, is not a very good choice if what you mean to stress is the importance of not deviating in any way from the liberal understanding of human rights. In my book I tried to show how it is possible to do justice to the intuition that human rights can neither be left to the sovereign legislative power nor simply converted into an instrument to be used for the latter's purposes. Private autonomy and citizens' autonomy mutually presuppose each other. And indeed the common origin of a people's sovereignty and human rights must be explained by the fact that citizens' practice of self-legislation in the form of institutionalized rights to political participation must be institutionalized; however, this presupposes the status of legal persons as bearers of subjective rights, and such a status-arrangement cannot exist without the classic rights to freedom. Without these rights, there is no positive law at all, and positive law happens to be the only language through which citizens can mutually assure each other of their participation in the practice of making their own laws.

153

The bilevel concept of society you presented in Theory of Communicative Action *afforded you an opportunity to diagnose and critique colonization of the life-world. Drawing on examples of the 'juridification' of communicatively structured realms of action, you show how, using monetary and bureaucratic means, the media-directed subsystems constituted by the economy and the state have made incursions into the symbolic reproduction of the life-world. The colonization thesis makes possible a critique of the medium of law. You seem to abandon this critique in* Between Facts and Norms. *What role if any do juridification tendencies continue to play in your critique of society? Have you given up the colonization thesis? What conceptual means does* Between Facts and Norms *make available to explain and criticize the negative effects of juridification in the realms of family, school, and social policy? And how, in this context, do you evaluate the shift of political decision making from parliament to the government and to the Federal Constitutional Court? For a democracy, doesn't this last development represent a threatening juridification of politics?*

I corrected myself on one point (cf. *Between Facts and Norms*). I no longer believe that juridification is an *inevitable* consequence of the welfare state. But juridification phenomena that I treat under the rubric 'welfare-state paternalism' continue to be relevant for me, because I want to show that today's return to the liberal model – praised as a 'society of private rights' – offers no way out of the dilemma constituted by the fact that when freedom is granted paternalistically, freedoms are simultaneously taken back. Starting from this way of framing the problems, I develop the proceduralist model of justice: in the complex relationships of the welfare state, private legal subjects cannot enjoy equal subjective freedoms if they fail, in their political role as co-legislators, to make use of their communicative freedoms by participating in public debates about how needs are to be interpreted, so that citizens themselves develop yardsticks and criteria according to which similar matters are treated similarly, and dissimilar matters dissimilarly.

So far as the juridification of politics itself is concerned, the constitutional court plays an unfortunate role to the extent that it exercises a subsidiary legislative function. The court ought not to confuse the constitution with a 'concrete order of values,' and in exercising its normative control it should essentially monitor the democratic character of the creation of laws; that is, it should ensure that the legislative process fulfills the exacting normative presuppositions of the democratic process. If our Federal Constitutional Court were to make such a proceduralist self-understanding the basis of its decisions, it could, for example, not simply send the abortion law back to the Bundestag, which had passed this law only after an exhaustive discursive preparation in the political public sphere and after repeated, conscientious consideration of all the arguments and counterarguments presented by all its members; moreover, it passed by a decisive, thoroughly bipartisan majority vote. At least the court ought not to have sent the law back unless it could produce *other* grounds for its decision.

The Federal Republic of Germany established a halfway reasonable democracy after 1945. In our opinion, basic rights and democratic institutions do not guarantee a properly functioning democracy. If citizens no longer perceive the possibility of participation, and have lost faith in politics – 'protest voters' and 'disgust with politics' are symptomatic of this – democracy is endangered. That is why in our view democratic learning processes – which are determined by historical experiences and education, among other things – are very important for a well-functioning democracy. In your essay 'The Second Lie of the Federal Republic: We're becoming Normal Again,' you speak of two 'life-lies' or collective self-deceptions that haunted the Federal Republic after 1945. The first originated during the Adenauer period: 'We are all democrats.' You claim that since 1989 a second life-lie has emerged: 'We have become normal again.' Could you explain to us what you mean by the 'second life-lie?' This is not immediately apparent to Scandinavians, who are not very well versed in German history. To what extent have these two lies diminished the democratic learning processes in the Federal Republic? Don't the years 1989–1990 mark a decisive break in this respect, because during the unification process the opportunity for a republican refounding of Germany was neglected?

I presume that the disgust with politics, which of course is not found solely in the Federal Republic, has different, contrary, and mutually reinforcing causes. On one hand, citizens are unhappy because they see too few opportunities to be meaningfully engaged politically along the well-trodden paths of a nationalized party landscape; the nonactivities of the local chapters of our political parties show how much unused energy is administered and laid to rest there. On the other hand, this wish for more democracy is intersected by the authoritarian wish to simplify an overly complex world by means of a simple recipe and strong men. The old stereotype of apolitically turning one's back on 'mere talk' *[Gerede]* and 'party squabbles' is receiving new impetus from fears about losses in income and status attributed to a politically out-of-control economic development that follows the pattern of 'jobless growth.' Clearly, politics has become overburdened by problems that are worldwide, and now also internally proliferating. It was not capitalism that won in the system competition with state Socialism but a capitalism that had been tamed by the welfare state during the favorable conjunctures of the postwar period, and which currently finds itself in a state of disintegration. This objectively difficult situation demands new solutions, but so far the imagination necessary to find them has been lacking.

It is against this general background that the Federal Republic has to digest the consequences of a precipitous annexation of the former GDR – a process conducted administratively and pushed through with confusing slogans. How far social disintegration will go, and how great the dangers it poses to internal stability will grow, no one can now say. In the general population, nationalist tendencies with regard to the internal German problems of distribution are not very marked. What we observe is an elite nationalism, cosponsored by intellectuals, which seeks to fill with backward-looking constructions the moral gap left by the anxiously avoided 1990 republican refounding. What worries me is that those who have always refused to acknowledge the political-cultural break of 1945 are the very ones who are now most loudly crying 'new normality' and 'goodbye to the old Federal Republic.' The political civilization of the Federal Republic made headway until 1989; the question is whether we will be able to continue this process in the enlarged Federal Republic – or whether the past will catch up with us again. One fortunate thing is that so far Kohl is stubbornly continuing to insist on a speedy unification to Europe.

In your article 'Citizenship and National Identity' you criticize the European Union's lack of democracy, but express 'cautiously optimistic expectations' (Between Facts and Norms) regarding European development. However, it seems much easier to internationalize democracy than to internationalize the economy and administration. The reason for your cautious optimism is not entirely clear to us. Doesn't the transnational character of an organization like the European Union make new demands on democracy? How extended and differentiated can a political public sphere be without completely exceeding the capacities of individual citizens faced with a highly complex society and the impossibility of gaining a comprehensive view of it? Can a radical democracy be realized within the framework of the EU at all?

We Germans need the political union if only to protect ourselves against the fantasies of 'a great eastward-looking power in the heart of Europe' that are beginning to be revived. For the same reason our neighbors should be interested in bringing Germany into mutual foreign and security policies. But that can be effectively done only within the framework of a common European constitution. So far, in Scandinavia and elsewhere opposition is directed only against a Brussels bureaucracy; that is, against a *systematically* created unity that still lacks a corresponding mutual political life-world, but such impulses might yet be able to translate themselves into a longing for a democratic Europe. The only genuine obstacle is the lack of a common political public sphere, the lack of an arena where subjects that have a *common relevance* can be negotiated. Ironically, whether such a communication context will develop depends on the intellectuals more than on another group, yet they go on endlessly arguing without doing anything to help.

6. Which History Can We Learn From?

1989 in the Shadow of 1945:
On the Normality
of a Future Berlin Republic

I

A NATION CELEBRATES as a day of liberation the day on which, after a war of conquest that lasted almost six years, it had to surrender unconditionally to the superior power of the opposing forces. This interpretation of 8 May 1945, which Friedrich von Weizäcker, who was then president of the Federal Republic, helped make officially accepted, reflects a retrospective recognition – but not a contemporary experience. Back in 1945, there was no resistance that could have triumphed. An elite's failed coup was not a civil war from which a victorious party could have emerged. Many individuals did feel liberated from the terror of the dictatorship, but this feeling was not representative of the mood of an overextended, exhausted population that had been driven into miserable wretchedness by disastrous battles, retreats, and destruction – a defeated population. Most people had long followed the slogan 'Ein Volk, ein Reich, ein Führer,' and they had by no means forgotten their complicity. For them, the end of the war at best signified a 'liberation' only in the psychological sense that a horrible end is better than a horror without end. Generally, 8 May was not experienced as a liberation in the political sense.

'1989 im Schatten von 1945. Zur Normalität einer künftigen Berliner Republik.' Address on the occasion of the fiftieth anniversary of the Nazi government's surrender (8 May 1945), given on 7 May 1995 in the Paulskirche in Frankfurt. Previously unpublished.

Yet we do not remember this day solely by mourning the victims of the barbarism perpetrated by our own nation, and ended by the Allies. Contrary to people's predominant experience at that time, we celebrate the day of the surrender with numerous public events, also taking a certain satisfaction in the turn toward something politically better. Of course, we cannot ignore the historical remove at which we stand from 1945; otherwise we will be tempted to project our interpretation back onto a people oppressed by the Nazis, onto our own youth, or onto our parents and grandparents. Neither can we hastily read the text of a liberation from fascism in relation to the justifying subtext of a worldwide civil war, in which 'we were always on the right side.' This line of thinking led to Bitburg. As citizens of an enlarged Federal Republic, we can make 8 May 1945 a 'day of liberation' and a starting point for political self-understanding only if we recognize that this retrospective interpretation resulted from a decades-long learning process.

This collective learning process was achieved differently and more easily in the Federal Republic than in the GDR. Taking the historical distance into account therefore requires fairness with regard to these differences. For example, how would things look if we compared the mass of Nazi fellow travelers who were quietly and rapidly reintegrated under Adenauer with the people on the other side of the border who bound up their socialist hopes – which were widely shared – with a Communist Party regime? Germans who found themselves to the west of the Soviet zone of occupation had drawn the better lot, and not only from a material point of view: the conditions for a change in their mentality were also objectively better.

The reestablishment of the democratic constitutional

state, the inclusion of the Federal Republic in the Western alliance, and the fundamental improvement in economic conditions were the major changes in direction. In addition, encumbrances that had still plagued the Weimar Republic were pushed aside: Prussian centralism, the imbalance and the split between religious denominations, the primacy and tradition-forming power of the military, and, above all, the political significance of elites rooted in traditional social structures. Moreover, the superpower lineup made for a beneficial primacy of interior politics, and the economic upswing of the period of reconstruction created a space for constructing and developing the welfare state. Finally, not only the loss of national sovereignty but also our own interests ultimately facilitated an energetically pursued integration into the European Economic Community. Thus, in an increasingly prosperous society, citizens were able to acquire confidence in their political order.

But the clear opportunity constituted by our ties to the West did not suffice to bring about a widespread transformation of this 'trust in the system' into a democratic mentality. Becoming accustomed to the advantages of a political and strategic dependence on the West had first to lead to a political culture oriented toward the West. German citizens had to be convinced of the normative substance of the political traditions developed in the West and rediscover the muted legacy of humanism and the Enlightenment in their own traditions. Because a republic ultimately can be stable only insofar as the principles of its constitution take root in the convictions and practices of its citizens. Such a mentality can be formed only within the context of a free and combative political culture; it emerges through criticism and confrontations in the arena of a public sphere that has not lost heart, is still accessible to arguments, and has not been ruined by commercial television. Such a network of motives and opinions, communicative forms and practices cannot be created with adminstrative means, and it constitutes the yardstick for measuring the political civilization of a community.

My thesis is that the Federal Republic has become politically civilized only to the degree that the obstacles to our perception of a heretofore unthinkable breach in civilization have been swept away. We had to learn to publicly confont a traumatic past. That a liberal political culture could develop in a culturally highly civilized society such as Germany only *after* Auschwitz is a truth difficult to grasp. The fact that it developed *because* of Auschwitz, because of reflection on the incomprehensible, is less difficult to understand if one considers what human rights and democracy mean at heart; namely, the simple expectation that no one will be excluded from the political community, and that the integrity of each individual, in his or her otherness, will be similarly respected.

II

Until 1989, we had good reason not to regard 1945 as a zero-point, but rather as a rupture in recent German history. Since 1989, many questions have been raised as to just how deep this rupture is. New German uncertainties are being connected with this date. The entry, on 3 October 1990, of the states emerging from the former GDR was not a republican refounding of the Federal Republic. Unification was not preceded by political self-understanding; there was no debate about the role of an enlarged Federal Republic or about what each side could legitimately expect from the other. This had both good and bad consequences. The elite nationalism of a handful of politicians and intellectuals found no response among the population, chiefly because the problems of distribution – which were hastily covered up, not dealt with in a way characterized by solidarity – continue to stimulate the enlightened self-interest of both sides. Even more burdensome is the effect on future generations of the resentment of the people in the east who feel administratively dismissed and devalued. In our context, a third consequence is the most important: essential questions of political self-understanding have remained open, especially the question as to how we should understand the 'normality' of the Berlin Republic that is advancing toward us.

The old Federal Republic had developed a certain sense for the dialectic of normalization; that is, a sense that only the avoidance of a self-satisfied, covering-up consciousness of 'normality' had allowed halfway normal conditions to emerge in our country. Is that supposed to end now? Do we have to revise our understanding of the rupture of 1945 in the light of the events of 1989–1990? Or was it after all in vain that an abysmal irony of history lent a highly ambivalent meaning to the date 9 November, which continues to be remembered here in the Paulskirche as the anniversary of the night of the [Kristallnacht] pogrom? Does 1989 remain for us Germans in the shadow of 1945 – for the time being – because it is only in light of the latter peripeteia that we can clearly understand the future of our political existence?

This can be understood as a question of historical punctuation. Historians write texts. The grammar of the narrative itself forces them to organize their sentences so that the succession of narrative events is articulated by commas, periods and paragraphs, and chapter divisions. This inevitably creates more-or-less deep ruptures, more-or-less close connections. Such retrospective divisions are relative – there are radically new beginnings only in art, not in history. But for the self-understanding of those who stand within traditions and who say 'yes,' or 'no,' and thus continue or interrupt these traditions, historical markers sometimes acquire the action-oriented quality of pivot points. Thus far, historical representations of our recent history have been distinguished from one another chiefly by their methodological starting points: oriented theoretically or narratively, toward social history or toward political or cultural history, toward structures or toward persons. However, the period around 1945 has constantly been seen as a pivot point. This seems to be changing. If I see matters correctly, two modes of revisionist reading that punctuate contemporary history in a different manner are becoming distinct.

For one mode of reading, national history provides the main thread. Seen from the perspective of the reestablishment of the nation-state, the continuities of the development since the founding of the Bismarck Reich are in the foreground. The nation divided in 1945 regained its normal form only in 1989. Hence the past fifty years look like a period during which Germany took a 'special path' ['Sonderweg'] and the Federal Republic eked out, in the shadow of world history, a Rhine-Union existence that was more or less agreeable but not to be taken entirely seriously. The main thread for the other reading is provided by Carl Schmitt's notion of the 'world civil war.' From the perspective of a battle waged against Bolshevism by the liberal West, the Nazi regime appears as only the vanguard, no matter how radical or degenerate, of a self-asserting occidental citizenship. The short-lived alliance against an encircled Germany is seen as a kind of misunderstanding that was cleared up by the realignments of the Cold War. At the end of the Cold

War, according to this view, the national history derailed in 1917 by totalitarianism fortunately got back on the normal track of development.

Both readings conclude that in 1989–1990 a shift from one historical era to another occurred that put an end to a transitory anomaly, evened out the break made in 1945, and beneficially relativized the apparent breach in civilization. This ensures the once again sovereign Germany a normal existence in central Europe, without 'fear of power.' The epochal threshold, which simultaneously paves the way for a return to a happier status quo ante, awakens a dialectical expectation: on the one hand, entirely new problems demand entirely new answers; on the other, these answers are to be mined from the sealed treasure trove of a tradition with which we made, in 1945, an 'infamous' break.

This may go a long way toward explaining the peculiar interest in things a hundred years old. I refer to the antiquarian curiosity about the conservative-revolutionary model of the very new in the very old, which of course still held the fascination of the entirely modern for the disenchanted generation of lieutenants returning home from World War I. Perhaps the murky mixture of a pulling-up-stakes mood with an end-of-the-world mood helps explain the analytic weakness and the diffuse emotionalism of an intellectual scene whose sloppy prattle, injustices tailored for the media, and neoconservative profundities do not even attempt to cover up the low level of public dialogue. The manipulation of the only half-understood expression 'political correctness' manifests a normative disinhibition and cognitive dedifferentiation in the treatment of sensitive issues. The critique of this newest Anglicism to enter the German language keeps raising the same point, which amounts to a polemic against so-called 'managing professionals.' The feature pages in the *Frankfurter Allgemeine* (see 13 January and 20 March 1995) share this tendency with the New Right, which is of course not so new. Shouldn't we breathe a sigh of relief when the federal president, in Dresden, masters a difficult situation without sounding the wrong notes?

Historians will ultimately answer the open question about how our contemporary history should be punctuated. To be sure, this punctuation shifts in accord with different hermeneutic starting points and with a particular present perspective on the future; these cannot be arbitrarily manipulated. But we cannot wait for the fourth volume of Hans Ulrich Wehler's study of German social history. Thus I will allow myself, as someone who is not a historian, a brief, more-or-less social-science-oriented, generalizing reflection on the achievements and limits of the nation-state. What we may have achieved with the successful refounding of the unity of a nation-state that was torn apart decades ago depends first of all on how we assess the future of the nation-state in general.

III

I want to develop the following thesis: the different tendencies toward the globalization of every kind of interchange and communication, economic production and its financing, transfers of technology and weaponry, the drug trade and criminality, and especially strategic and ecological dangers, confront us with problems that can no longer be solved within the framework of the nation-state. The hollowing-out of the sovereignty of the nation-state will continue, and require us to develop capacities for political action on a supranational basis. On the other hand, 'globalization' represents a step toward abstraction that threatens to dissolve the social glue that holds together already fragmented national societies. This step along the road to abstraction continues a process with which European modernity has made us familiar. At one time, the organizational form of the nation-state provided a convincing response to the demand for a new form of social integration. This suggests that if we are now to follow willingly and consciously the path that leads toward postnational societies, we should take the integrational achievements of the nation-state as our guide. Otherwise, new organizations will emerge, and the constitutional state and democracy will fall by the wayside.

As the name 'United Nations' already shows, world society today is divided into nation-states that recognize each other as subjects in international law. The historical nation-state that emerged in western and northern Europe and from the American and French Revolutions has spread throughout the world. It was superior to its competitors, to the city-states and city leagues as well as to the modern successors of the old empires – we are now witnessing the transformation of China, the last empire of this kind. This success of the nation-state naturally derives first of all from the advantages of the modern state *as such*. The administrative and taxation state that monopolizes power has by and large left the tasks of production to an economy differentiated from the state; and that is what made this tandem – bureaucratic state and capitalist economy – into the driving force of social modernization.

Today, we all live in national societies that owe their unity to a state organized in this way. Such states of course existed long before there were 'nations' in the modern sense of the word. State and nation coalesced into a nation-state only after the French Revolution. What is peculiar to this combination? Let me here interpret interconnected processes, which persisted throughout the nineteenth century, on the basis of their end result, and bring them under a common denominator. The 'invention of the people's nation' (H. Schulze) had a catalyzing effect on the democratization of state power. A democratic basis for the legitimation of domination would not have developed without national self-awareness, because it was the nation that first created solidarity between persons who until then had been strangers to each other. (The German expression *Solidarzuschlag*, which refers to an additional tax to pay for solidarity with the east, is related to that conceptual history.) The achievement of the nation-state thus consists in having simultaneously solved two problems: it makes possible a new mode of legitimation through a new form of social integration.

To put it crudely, the legitimation problem arose from the fact that the schism in religion led to the privatization of faith, with the result that power's religious grounding in divine grace also gradually disappeared. The secularized state had to find its justification elsewhere. The problem of social integration depended – and this is just as crude a simplification – on urbanization and economic modernization, on the extension and acceleration of exchange in goods, persons, and information: the population was torn out of the corporative social groups in early modern society and at the same time mobilized and individualized. The nation-state responded to both these challenges by politically mobilizing its citizens; that is, it coupled a more abstract form of social integration with changed political decision-making structures: subjects of the crown became citizens of the state. A gradual assertion of democratic participation provides citizens with a new level of social connectedness and simultaneously secures for the state a secular source of legitimation. However, we need to keep separate two aspects of this reformation of the state – the political-legal aspect and the properly cultural aspect.

The state was already constituted in the forms of positive law, and it made use of this medium to organize social intercourse in such a way that private individuals were able to enjoy subjective rights – which were at first unequally distributed. With the organizational form of (developing) bourgeois civil law, the citizens of a society, as Kant still put it, had already obtained, in their role as 'subjects of the crown' [Untertanen], an element of private autonomy. In the course of the transformation of the ruler's sovereignty into people's sovereignty, the paternalistically granted rights of subjects are transformed into human rights and citizens' rights. Along with private autonomy, these rights now guarantee political autonomy – in principle, for everyone alike. In this way, out of the territorial state emerges the democratic consitutional state; that is, the idea of an order chosen by the people itself and legitimated by democratic will-formation, in which those who are subject to the law can also consider themselves its authors.

But such a legal-political reorganization would have lacked driving force had those who were defined from above as 'the people' not become a nation of self-confident citizens. This political mobilization required an idea with consensus-building power that could appeal more strongly to hearts and minds than could the ideas of a people's sovereignty and human rights by themselves. This need is filled by the idea of a nation; it is this idea that first makes the inhabitants of a state's territory aware of a new, politically mediated form of belonging together. It is national self-awareness – which crystallizes around a common origin, language, and history, the sense of belonging to a people – that first makes subjects into citizens, that makes them feel that they belong to the same political community and feel responsible *for each another*. The nation or spirit of the people – the first modern form of collective identity – thus provides the cultural base for the legal organizational unity of the state. Historians describe the artificial, propagandistically directed transformation of the 'nation' under a ruler into a nation of the people as a long-term change in consciousness inspired by intellectuals and scholars, which first asserts itself among the educated urban middle class before finding a reponse among the people as a whole.

IV

However, the price the nation-state pays for these advantages is an ambivalent self-understanding. For the idea of the nation is bound up with the Machiavellian will to self-assertion, which from the outset the sovereign state has allowed to lead it into the arena of the great powers. Along with the two egalitarian concepts of freedom – that of the private freedom of the citizen of a society and the political autonomy of the citizen of a state – a third concept comes into play: the entirely different *particularist* concept of national freedom. This refers to the independence of one's own nation, which must be defended, if need be, with the 'blood of its sons.' As compared with the republican freedoms of individuals, this collective freedom is the place where the secularized state retains a nonsecularized remnant of transcendence. The warring nation-state requires its citizens to risk their lives for the collective good: 'Sacrifice for the individuality of the state is the substantial relationship of all, and thus the duty of all' (Hegel, *Philosophy of Right*, ¶ 325). General military duty has been the flip side of citizens' rights ever since the French Revolution; the willingness to fight and die for the fatherland is supposed to prove both national consciousness and republican consensus.

This double coding also manifests itself in inscriptions of historical memories: the milestones in the fight for republican freedoms are linked with the death symbolism of commemorative ceremonies honoring those who fell on the battlefield. This double 'memory' trace reflects the twofold nature of the nation – the desired nation of citizens, which creates democratic legitimation, as well as the born nation of *Volksgenossen*, which makes for national integration. *Citizens* constitute themselves on their own as a political association of the free and equal; *Volksgenossen* see themselves as belonging to an ethnic community bound together by a common language and historical destiny. The tension between the universalism of an egalitarian community under law and the particularism of a historical community of destiny is built into the nation-state.

These two elements mesh seamlessly only when the completely secularized state no longer assumes the right to determine the life and death of its citizens in the name of the collective (that is, when it eliminates the death penalty and general conscription). Then the republican idea can take the lead, penetrating and structuring socially integrative life-forms. Conversely, the republic is damaged if the integrative strength of a nation is based on a prepolitical given, on a fact independent of the formation of political will. A nation *naturalized* in this way replaces the historical contingency of the contextualizing of the community and fortifies artificially created boundaries by lending them the aura of the natural. Although a people's nation [*Volksnation*] is largely an artifact, it imagines itself to have grown organically and understands itself by contrast with the artificial order of positive law.

The history of imperialism between 1871 and 1914, and even more the all-encompassing nationalism of the twentieth century, prove that the idea of the nation has unfolded its mobilizing power almost exclusively in its particularistic form. This source of energy was exhausted in Germany only after the rupture of 1945. Only when the European powers, under the nuclear umbrella of the superpowers, were denied the exercise of their own foreign policy did the self-understanding of the democratic, legally constituted state detach itself, not only in theory but also within the population at large, from the patterns of national self-assertion and geopolitical power politics. Domestic social conflicts thus could also now be worked on in a situation where domestic politics was primary. This tendency toward a certain 'postnationalist' self-understanding on the part of the political community may have asserted itself more strongly in the special situation of the Federal Republic, which had been deprived of the essential rights of sovereignty, than it did in other states. But the pacification of class antagonism through the welfare state produced a new situation in all these countries. During the postwar period, social security systems, along with reforms in education, family and penal law, data protection, and so on, were developed, and the first steps toward equal status for women were taken. Although it is still incomplete, the status of the citizen has gained a broader legal substance. This achievement – and that is what matters to me here – has made the citizens themselves aware of the *primacy* of the achievement of basic rights – of the primacy of the actual nation of citizens, which, if it is not to fail, must be upheld over an imaginary nation of *Volksgenossen*.

The great thing about republicanism is that the democratic process simultaneously assumes responsibility for breakdowns in the social integration of a more and more differentiated society. In a culturally pluralistic society with many different worldviews this burden cannot simply be shifted from the level of political will-formation and public communication to the apparently naturally developed substratum constituted by an allegedly homogeneous people. Behind that facade is concealed nothing other than a hegemonic majority culture. But the latter must be extricated from its fusion with a *political* culture shared by *all* citizens if different cultural, religious, and ethnic life-forms are to coexist with equal rights within the same community. In that respect, classic immigration countries such as the United States are ahead of us; there, everyone can live with two identities, simultaneously belonging to the country and being a foreigner in it.

From the conflict-ridden and painful processes of making the transition to a multicultural society emerges a form of social integration that already points beyond the nation-state. The formation of nations is repeated on a more abstract level: the structures of political decision making acquire a new cultural substrate. For once again it is political and cultural integration, the common attachment to historically achieved republican freedoms, once again it is loyalty to a convincing political order anchored in historical consciousness, that motivate citizens, above and beyond their subcultural differences, to assume mutual responsibility for each other.

Republicanism realizes its true nature to the extent that it shakes off the ambivalent potential of nationalism, which once served as its vehicle. The multicultural form of social integration that has been hatched under the wing of the nation-state must still prove itself outside and beyond the nation-state. For example, the states growing together under the umbrella of the European Union must still develop a common political culture. Before a European constitution can take hold, a public sphere extending throughout Europe must be formed, which will allow its citizens, and not just its governments, to take part in a common process of shaping a political will. Many people regard that as a mere utopia. But the very global problems today that are now overwhelming us and arousing skepticism are also driving us, for reasons of our own self-interest, in precisely this direction.

V

The nation-state guarded its territorial and social boundaries in an almost neurotic manner. Today it is challenged by global tendencies that do not respect borders and have already perforated them. A. Giddens has defined 'globalization' as the intensification of worldwide relationships, with the result that local and far-distant events mutually affect each other. Worldwide physical, social, and symbolic contacts are produced via space-spanning, accelerated connections, chiefly electronic. These communications are conducted in natural languages or by means of special codes – by means of money, for example. They promote the expansion of the consciousness of the actors on the one hand, and the branching out, extension, and connection of systems, networks, and organizations. This process creates two contrary tendencies – the simultaneous *expansion* and *frag-*

mentation of the consciousness of planning subjects who are communicating and acting with one another.

If the manifold forms of communication are not to spread out centrifugally and be lost in global villages, but rather foster a focused process of shaping will and opinion, public spheres must be created. Participants must be able simultaneously to exchange contributions on the same subjects of the same relevance. It was through this kind of communication – at that time conducted by literary means – that the nation-state knitted together a new network of solidarity, which enabled it to some extent to head off modernism's drive to abstraction and to re-embed a population torn out of traditional life-relationships in the contexts of expanded and rationalized life-worlds. Confronted by the drive to abstraction that has occurred since then, we must ask whether the republican idea of a society's conscious intervention in its own development can still be politically institutionalized. The question is whether a public consciousness that is expanding but centered on the life-world is still capable of spanning systematically differentiated relationships, or whether now independent, systemic courses of events have long since disconnected all the connections that political communication produces.

Skeptical answers to this question are currently dominant. Their general tenor is that the end of the nation-state means the end of any kind of normatively demanding political socialization. In this postpolitical world, transnational enterprises become the behavioral model. J. M. Guéhenno describes the 'end of democracy' from the perspective of citizens who have been dismissed from the liquidated context of the state's solidarist community. Without any illusions, they must find their way in a fractured world of free-floating and self-asserting systems, of which they can gain no overview; on their own, all they have left to guide themselves are rules for making as rational a choice as possible among systemically produced options. In a world of anonymously networked relationships they operate on global markets with – so to speak – an economically local consciousness. The neoliberal core of this vision is ultradistinct. The autonomy of citizens, abandoned to processes of the world economy, which have become incomprehensible but are somehow spontaneously regulated by a 'logic of the network,' is without further ado shorn of its state-citizen component and reduced to a private autonomy.

But the well-known examples of such mechanisms of self-regulation do not exactly inspire trust. The 'balance of power' on which the international system depended for three hundred years broke down with World War II at the latest. The founding of the UN signified a second attempt to build up supranational means for taking action in the interest of a peacable global order that still remains to be realized. And the world market – the other example of spontaneous networking – clearly cannot be left at the discretion of the World Bank and the International Monetary Fund, if we are ever to overcome the asymmetrical interdependence between the OECD world and marginalized countries that must still develop self-sufficient economies. The bill the world social summit in Copenhagen has just handed us is devastating. Supranational means of taking action on ecological problems whose global interrelationship was negotiated at the world summit in Rio de Janeiro are conspicuously lacking. A world order and a world economic order that are more peaceful and more just are unimaginable without international institutions capable of action, and especially without voting procedures, among regional regimes currently caught up in development, in the framework and under the pressure of a worldwide, mobile civil society.

The lack of supranational authorities capable of acting on the global system in accord with a coordinated world domestic policy is also becoming noticeable here at home. The debates about our standpoint we are currently conducting make us aware of the gap opening up between the arena of action marked off by the nation-state and the imperatives, not so much of world trade, as of globally networked conditions of production. Capitalism has certainly developed in worldwide dimensions from the outset. For centuries, the dynamics of economic development that was set free within the system of European states has been growing stronger. Sovereign states can also live comfortably with free trade zones. But they profit from their various economies only so long as these are 'people's economies' ['Volkswirtschaften'] that they can influence indirectly by political means. However, with the denationalization of the economy, and especially of the worldwide networking of the financial markets with industrial production itself, national politics loses its power over the general conditions of production. Governments find themselves under increasing pressure to accept higher rates of permanent unemployment as the price for being able to compete internationally, and not merely to reconstruct but largely to dismantle the welfare state. Today the elimination of public pensions and medical insurance is already being proposed. However, those who make this argument must be prepared to live with an underclass in their own country.

The 'underclass' is what sociologists call that bundle of marginalized groups that are largely cut off – 'segmented' –

from the rest of society. Those who can no longer change their social situation on their own have fallen out of the solidarist context of state citizenship. They can no longer pose any kind of threat – any more than the former Third World can threaten the First. However, segmentation does not mean that a political community can simply split off one of its parts *without consequences.* As can already be seen elsewhere, in the long run at least three consequences are inevitable. An underclass creates social tensions that are discharged in aimless, self-destructive revolts, which can be controlled only by repressive means. Building prisons, and organizing internal security in general, becomes a growth industry. Moreover, social neglect and physical misery cannot be limited to a given location. The poison in the ghettos attacks the infrastructure of the inner cities, indeed of entire regions, and lodges firmly in the pores of the whole society. This ultimately results in the moral erosion of the society, something that must harm the core of every republican community. Majority decisions achieved in a formally correct manner, but which reflect only the status-anxieties and self-assertive reflexes of a middle class threatened with decline, undermine the legitimacy of the procedures and institutions of the constitutional state and of democracy.

Anyone who replies to the signals of such a desolidarization with an appeal to the 'self-confident nation,' or by calling for a return to the 'normality' of the reestablished national state, is using the devil to drive out Satan. For these unsolved global problems reveal precisely the *limits* of the nation-state. From the somber drumroll of national history emerge war memorials with limited vision. Only as a critical authority does history serve as a teacher. At best, it tells us how we ought *not* to do it. It is from experiences of a negative kind that we learn. That is why 1989 will remain a fortunate date only so long as we respect 1945 as the genuinely instructive one.

Today we must try to carry further the legacy of the nation-state on a European level. A Berlin republic without the fatal aftertaste of the wrong continuities would in fact operate less autonomously, and yet with greater initiative, than the old Federal Republic. It would not, looking eastward, project itself as a sovereign supreme power, but would act in a focused manner. It would make its influence felt within the institutional framework of a democratically developed European Union and work to ensure that, together, Europeans live up to their responsibility outside as well as within Europe. As part of a greater whole that must be characterized by solidarity, this republic would no longer arouse its neighbors' suspicion about the super-mark and great-power aspirations. Instead of issuing saber-rattling decisions from Berlin, it would have to win majorities in Strasbourg and Brussels. Disencumbered in this way, it would not need to shy away from taking the long view. It could work on operationalizing long-range objectives that could provide motivational impulses once they are no longer suspected of being utopian. Europeans bear responsibility, not only for making the organization of the community of peoples [Völkergemeinschaft] finally fit to undertake a cooperative solution of global problems that are becoming increasingly insoluble, but also for halting within their own societies the decline of existing social standards, as well as the division that results from the chauvinism of affluence.

Index

Abendroth, Wolfgang, 102, 115
abortion, xxii, 84, 155
Academia Moralis, 110–11
Adenauer regime, xiii, 29–30, 80,
  88, 102, 156, 162
Adorno, Gretel, 119, 120
Adorno, Theodor, xii–xiv, xviii–
  xx, xxiii, 17–18, 19, 35, 41, 59,
  60, 69, 70, 87, 91, 102, 103,
  119–27
Altmann, Rüdiger, 113
Apel, Karl-Otto, xx, 148
Arendt, Hannah, xii, 119, 143,
  144
Arndt, Hans-Joachim, 110
Aristotle, 18
asylum, right of, xv, xxi, 1, 65–66,
  69, 84, 151, 152
Auschwitz, 25, 53, 97, 164

Barion, Hans, 111, 112
Basic Law, German, 89–90, 116
Bataille, Georges, 123, 124
Benjamin, Walter, xii, xiii, 119–27;
  'Arcades' book (Passagenarbeit),
  122–23, 125
Benn, Gottfried, 111
Bidenkopf, Kurt, 35
Biermann, Wolf, 29, 91
Bloch, Ernst, 121, 134
Böckenförde, Ernst-Wolfgang, 113
Bohrer, Karl Heinz, 113

Boveri, Margret, 111
Brecht, Bertolt, 121
Buchenwald, 22
Bundestag Investigative Commis-
  sion, 33, 34, 39, 41–56

Callois, Roger, 124
capitalism, 13, 62–63, 64, 71, 87,
  135, 140–42, 157, 169, 179; and
  democracy, 139–42
Citizens' Rights movement, 26,
  31, 37, 43, 50, 51, 142
civil society, xxii, 142–45
class antagonism, 174
Cold War, 166–67; end of, 131
communication, ix, xvii, xviii,
  xix–xx, 61, 71, 77, 84–85, 133,
  134–36, 143–44, 155, 176; ideal
  communication community,
  145–49
Conze, Werner, 112
Cortez, Donoso, 108
Critical Theory, xiii, xviii, xix,
  69–70, 103

Dahrendorf, Ralf, xiii, 88
Darwin, Charles, 86
debate, public, 19–20, 34–35
democracy, ix–xi, xv–xvii, xx–
  xxiv, 41–44, 49–51, 77–78,
  131–49, 155–58, 164, 171;
  radical, ix, x, xv–xvi, xviii, xxi,

democracy (*continued*)
xxiii, 74, 88, 92, 131, 132–34,
136–37
Dewey, John, 102
Dieckmann, Friedrich, 99
Dilthey, Wilhelm, 8
Durkheim, Émile, 102
Dworkin, Ronald, 73, 102

Eastern Europe, 21, 24, 55, 63
economic disparity, 13, 62, 64, 98,
139–42, 179–180, 181
Enlightenment, xi, xii, 59, 60, 61,
98, 102, 108, 127, 163
environmental issues, 63, 64, 131,
140–42, 168, 178
Enzensberger, Hans Magnus, 91,
113
Eppelmann, Rainer, 33
Erhard, Ludwig, 9
ethnic conflict, 13, 62
Eurocentrism, 85–86
European unification (European
Union), xviii, xxiii, 39, 55, 62,
66–67, 157, 158, 163, 176, 181

Fack, Fritz Ullrich, 28
Federal Republic of Germany. *See*
Germany; Germany, West
Forsthof, Ernst, 111
47 Group, 29
Foucault, Michel, 147, 148
France, 64, 65
Frankfurter Allgemeine Zeitung,
xiv, 5, 28, 45, 81, 89, 116, 127,
168
Frankfurt School, xii, xix, 87,
103
freedom, collective vs. individual,
172–73

Freud, Sigmund, 17, 18, 86, 102,
127
Freyer, Hans, 81, 111
Fukuyama, Francis, 131

Gadamer, Hans Georg, 8
Gehlen, Arnold, 69, 81, 83, 112
German Democratic Republic
(GDR): economic development
of, 9, 21; intellectuals in, xiv,
26, 37, 64–65, 95–105; law
of, 30
German mandarinism, 12, 60, 83,
101
German past, xiii, 1, 5, 11–13, 21–
56, 89, 90–91, 97, 161–68; and
1989, xi, xvi, 12, 54, 164–67, 181;
and 1945, x, xii, xiii, xvi, 12, 54,
114–15, 116, 161–62, 164–67, 181;
and two dictatorships (double
past), 21–30, 40, 41, 44–51, 53,
55, 97; 'working off' of, 17–40,
41–44, 84, 96, 104
Germany: courts of, xxii–xxiii,
73–74, 155; differences between
East and West, 38–40, 48–49,
100, 101, 162, 165; foreign policy
of, xiv, 66–67; intellectuals
in, 11–12, 64–65, 96, 107–17,
126, 157, 164, 167; national
identity of, 90–91; nationalism
in, xvi, xvii, 157, 164–65; and
'normalization,' 1, 22, 39, 109,
127, 156–57, 165; and opening to
Western traditions, x–xi, 66, 81,
88–89, 101, 102, 126–27, 163–
64; reunification of, xi, xiv, xvi,
13, 21–22, 27, 35, 40, 64–65, 96,
98, 99, 156–57, 164; traditions
of, ix, xi, xii–xiii, 103, 126, 127

Index

Germany, West (Federal Republic): affected by unification, xiv, 22–23, 44, 96, 162–64; and 'normalization,' 165; intellectuals in, 95–105

Gulf War, 1, 13, 23

Giddens, A., 176

globalization, xvii, 85, 141–42, 149, 168–72, 176–81

Gorz, André, 140

Grass, Günter, 38

Gross, Johannes, 113

Guéhenno, J. M., 177, xvii

Habermas, Jurgen: *Between Facts and Norms,* xxii, 71, 74, 88, 131, 132, 134–35, 140, 145, 147, 151, 154, 158; *Die Integration moderner Gesellschaften,* 147; *Knowledge and Human Interest,* vii; *The Past as Future,* 99; 'The Second Lie of the Federal Republic,' 156; *The Structural Transformation of the Public Sphere,* vii, viii, x; *Theory of Communicative Action,* vii, 71, 86, 84, 134–35, 138, 139, 140, 147, 154; *Volkssouveränität als Verfahren,* 134

'hawks' and 'doves,' 35–38, 40

Hegel, G. W. F., 7, 8, 10, 83, 86, 102, 173

Heidegger, Martin, xi, 32, 39, 59, 60, 81, 83, 91, 103, 107–9, 111, 115, 122

Heidenreich, Gerd, 40

Heine, Heinrich, 127

Henrich, Dieter, 100

Heitmann, Klaus 5

Historia Magistra Vitae, 6, 9

Historians' Controversy, xiv, 22, 88, 97

history: xi, xiv, 5–13, 24, 43–44, 52–55, 76, 91, 165–68, 173, 180–81

Hitler, Adolf, xi, 23, 27, 51, 108, 117

Horkheimer, Max, xii, xviii, 103, 119, 125

homelessness, 13

humanism, 103, 108, 163

immigration, xvi, 55, 62–63, 65, 82, 98

intellectual, role of, viii, ix, xxiii, 31, 55, 84, 158, 172

Jäckel, Eberhard, 24, 26, 47

Jaspers, Karl, 29, 108

Jens, Walter, 38

Jordan, Pascual, 112

Jung, C. G., 124, 125

Jünger, Ernst, 81, 103, 111

justice: political, 20, 28, 30–34, 36, 38, 49–51, 98

Kafka, Franz, 127

Kambartel, Friedrich, 140

Kant, Immanuel, x, 10, 61, 78, 83, 84, 102, 127, 135, 171

Kesting, Hanno, 112, 113, 114

Kierkegaard, Sören, 18, 86

Klages, Ludwig, 124

Klee, Ernst, 28

Klein, Felix, 9

Kluge, Alexander, 70

Kogon, Eugen, 29, 32

Kohl, Helmut, 157

Koselleck, Reinhart, 5, 6, 113

Kracauer, Siegfried, 120

Kraus, Karl, 127

Index

Krauss, Gunther, 111

law: xxii–xxiii, xv, 20–21, 42–43, 71–72, 73, 74, 88, 112, 132–33, 135–36, 149; juridification, 154–55; positive law, xxi–xxii, 72, 73, 102, 145, 153, 171
Left (political), x, 46–47, 81, 91, 96, 99; New Left, xiii
Leiris, Michel, 124
Lenin, V. I., 9, 23
Le Pen, Jean-Marie, 143, 145
Lepenies, Wolf, 21, 26
Liebknecht, Karl, 23
life-world, viii, xxii, xxiii, 71, 76, 77, 79, 83, 84, 87, 92, 139, 140, 141, 142, 145, 147, 154, 177
Löwenthal, Leo, xii, 121
Lübbe, Hermann, 113
Luhmann, Niklas, 148
Lukács, Georg, 102, 103–4

Maizière, Lothar de, 22
Marcuse, Herbert, xii, 121
Marx, Karl, 7, 8, 26, 86–87, 102, 127, 141, 150
mass media, 20, 32, 75–76, 144–45, 164
Maunz, Theodor, xii, 116, 117
modernism (modernity), xi, 60–61, 70, 80, 83, 87, 103, 123–24, 125, 126, 132, 169, 177
Mohler, Armin, 81, 110
morality, 71–72, 73
Müller, Heiner, 127

nation-state, xvi–xvii, 141, 168–72, 172–81
nationalism, xvii–xviii, 53, 62, 145, 174, 176

Nietzsche, Friedrich, 8, 86, 108
Noack, Paul, 117
Nolte, Ernst, xi, 23–24, 89, 107

Offe, Claus, 140

Parsons, Talcott, 102
personalization, 20–21, 32–33, 38
Peters, Bernhard, 147
philosophy, xviii–xx, 59–61, 83–87, 121–25
Pierce, Charles Sanders, xx, 86, 102, 148
Positivism Debate, 88
poverty, 131, 143
private sphere, xxii, 32, 76, 77, 105, 133
public sphere, vii, viii, ix, x, xii, xv, xvi, xvii, xxi, xxiii, 20, 32, 52, 53, 77, 108, 133, 137, 142–45, 147, 149–50, 163–64, 176, 177
Putnam, Hilary, 148

racism, 66, 131
Ranke, Leopold von, 7
rationalism, xx, xix, 86
Ravensbrück, 22
Rawls, John, 78, 102, 132, 135
reason, xix, 59, 60–61, 84
Reich, Jens, 95
republicanism, 173–76
reunification. See Germany, reunification of
Right (political), 23, 46–47, 80–81, 89, 91–92, 96–97, 99, 107, 113; radicalism of, 13, 66, 78, 96–97; neoconservative intellectuals, ix, xvi, 127
rights: democratic, xiv; basic, 140, 151–53; human, xxi–xxii, xxiii,

24–25, 85–86, 112, 151–53, 164,
171; citizens', xxi, 46, 150–53,
171
Ritter, Joachim, 112

Schapiro, Meyer, 119
Schäuble, Wolfgang, 5, 96, 105
Scheibert, Peter, 111
Schelsky, Helmut, 111
Schiller, Johann, 7
Scholem, Gershom, 119, 121,
122
Schmitt, Carl, ix, xi, 32, 45, 81,
90, 91, 103, 107–17, 166
Schnur, Roman, 113
Schoenberg, Arnold, 127
Schöllgen, Gregor, 82
Schönhuber, Franz, 143, 145
Schorlemmer, Friedrich, 30, 31,
32, 38–39, 96
Schröder, Richard, 99
Schulze, H., 170
self-understanding, 18–21, 29, 31,
33, 34, 38, 39, 42, 50, 51, 53,
55–56, 62, 65, 91, 105, 112, 145,
162, 165, 172
Sieburg, Friedrich, 80
Sombart, Nicolaus, 112, 114
Soviet Union, 12, 24, 91, 92
Spaeman, Robert, 113
Stalin, Joseph, 23
Stapel, Wilhelm, 111
state Socialism, x, 26, 62, 91, 92,
139–42, 157
Stolpe case, 25, 38, 50
Strauß, Botho, 91, 113, 127
Stürmer, Michael, 5, 13
Syberberg, Hans Jurgen, 127

Taylor, Charles, 79

technology, and democracy,
137–39
Templin, Wolfgang, 32
Thierse, Wolfgang, 31, 32, 35, 40
Third World, 63, 180
tradition, 8–9, 10–11, 12, 19, 44,
49, 55, 76
tribunalization, 20–21, 31, 38
Trotzky, Leon, 23

Ullmann, Wolfgang, 31, 32
unemployment, 13, 179
United Nations (UN), 55, 63, 67,
69, 82, 142, 152, 169, 178
United States, x, 62, 98, 120, 175
universalism, 78, 85

von Beyme, Klaus, 136

Walser, Martin, 91, 100
Walzer, Michael, 79
Weber, Max, xix, 60
Weber, Werner, 111
Wehler, Hans Ulrich, 168
Weissman, Karl-Heinz, 82
von Weizäcker, Friedrich, 161
welfare state, 71, 98, 142, 154–55,
157, 174, 179
Wellmer, Albrecht, 103, 126, 146,
148
Wieacker, Franz, 112
Willms, Bernard, 81, 110
Wirsting, Giselher, 111
Wolf, Christa, xi, 34, 95–105
workers' movement, European,
63, 98

xenophobia, xiv–xv, 65, 145

Zehrer, Hans, 111

In the *Modern
German Culture and Literature*
series

*Making Bodies, Making
History: Feminism and German Identity*
By Leslie A. Adelson

*The Powers of Speech:
The Politics of Culture in the* GDR
By David Bathrick

*The Institutions of Art:
Essays by Peter Bürger and Christa Bürger*
Translated by Loren Kruger

A Berlin Republic: Writings on Germany
By Jürgen Habermas
Translated by Steven Rendall
Introduction by Peter Uwe Hohendahl

The Past as Future
By Jürgen Habermas Interviewed
by Michael Haller
Translated and edited by Max Pensky

*The Cinema's Third Machine:
Writing on Film in Germany, 1907–1933*
By Sabine Hake

*The Soul of Wit:
Joke Theory from Grimm to Freud*
By Carl Hill

*A History of German Literary Criticism,
1730–1980*
Edited by Peter Uwe Hohendahl

Prismatic Thought: Theodor W. Adorno
By Peter Uwe Hohendahl

Bertolt Brecht and the Theory of Media
By Roswitha Mueller

*Toward a Theory of Radical
Origin: Essays on
Modern German Thought*
By John Pizer

*Art and Enlightenment:
Aesthetic Theory after Adorno*
By David Roberts

*East, West, and Others:
The Third World in Postwar
German Literature*
By Arlene A. Teraoka

*'All Power to the Imagination!'
The West German Counterculture
from the Student Movement
to the Greens*
By Sabine von Dirke